G000066604

The Social Determinants of Mental Health:
From Awareness to Action

Exploring the ways social context impacts mental health and well-being

Adler Institute on Social Exclusion
ANNUAL CONFERENCE

Conference Proceedings

The Drake Hotel
CHICAGO, ILLINOIS

June 3-4, 2010

Table of Contents

Table of Contents

Introduction

On June 3-4, 2010, more than 230 people from the United States, Canada, the United Kingdom, Portugal, Peru, Thailand, and Bermuda attended the annual conference of the Adler Institute on Social Exclusion (ISE). Entitled "The Social Determinants of Mental Health: From Awareness to Action," this gathering was held at The Drake Hotel in downtown Chicago. Before the conference began, an event entitled "Violence as a Social Determinant of Mental Health," took place on June 2 and featured Carl Bell, M.D., director of Public and Community Psychiatry at the University of Illinois at Chicago, as well as a presentation by staff of the Office of Violence Prevention from the Chicago Department of Public Health.

This conference was the first in the United States to convene thinkers and practitioners from diverse backgrounds for the purpose of understanding and effectively addressing the social determinants of health. It is widely understood that social conditions impact physical health, often leading to higher than average rates of respiratory, cardiovascular, and infectious diseases, as well as cancers and diabetes. Less attention has been directed toward the ways in which social conditions impact mental health. Attendees of the groundbreaking conference came to increase their awareness and understanding of how social conditions determine mental health and well-being, and to hear about some of the innovative prevention strategies that are informed by the social determinants framework.

One of the key messages of the conference was the importance of collaboration and the establishment of 'unlikely alliances' among diverse sectors (e.g., housing, transportation, public health, education, economic development, and law enforcement) and professions (e.g., policy makers, academics, and service providers). Since those sectors involve decisions and actions that shape the social environment, they necessarily contribute to mental health.

The conference featured a diverse range of presenters, including keynote speaker David Satcher, M.D., Ph.D., who was the 16th Surgeon General of the United States, a director of the Centers for Disease Control and Prevention, and a member of the World Health Organization (WHO) Commission on the Social Determinants of Health.

In his remarks, Dr. Satcher called for a 'global movement' to eliminate health disparities by addressing the social determinants of health. "We need a movement that places fair health, fair distribution of health, and better overall population health at the head and heart of governance," said Dr. Satcher. "Is health – including mental health – about personal responsibility? Yes and no. Communities have to have places to be safely active and to buy good foods. We must focus on personal responsibility and social responsibility and integrate both."

Dr. Satcher was followed by a distinguished panel of speakers including Gail C. Christopher, D.N., Vice President for Programs, Food, Health, and Well-Being, at the W.K. Kellogg Foundation; Aida Giachello, Ph.D., Director, Midwest Latino Health Research, Training and Policy Center at the University of Illinois at Chicago; Terry Mason, M.D., the Chief Medical Officer of the Cook County Health System (Metropolitan Chicago); and Aaron Wernham, M.D., is the Director of the Health Impact Project at The Pew Health Group, Pew Charitable Trusts.

The panel was moderated by Marian McDonald, Associate Director of Health Disparities, National Center for Emerging and Zoonotic Infectious Diseases, Centers for Disease Control and Prevention. Each of the panelists spoke about the various ways in which the social environment impacts mental health and the importance of addressing those social determinants of mental health.

The conference also featured more than 25 oral, art, and poster presentations. Presenters came from a variety of disciplines, including public health, psychology, psychiatry, sociology, anthropology, law, and philosophy. Public officials, foundation executives, and members of the academic and non-profit communities also participated. They addressed such topics as food security, immigration and refugee policy, employment status, economic conditions, and violence. They also discussed the social determinants of adolescent depression and suicide, as well as the determinants of the mental health of sexual, racial, and ethnic minorities. Furthermore, speakers described some of the intervention and prevention strategies available to address the ways the social environment impacts mental health.

Speakers and attendees emphasized the importance of keeping the momentum of the conference going. In this regard, Sandro Galea, M.D., M.P.H., Dr.P.H., a noted social epidemiologist, said, "An institution, such as the Adler School, can be quite powerful in pushing awareness of and action on the social determinants of mental health, and in leading the way forward." Dr. Galea, who is Gelman Professor and Chair of the Department of Epidemiology at the Columbia University's Mailman School of Public Health in New York, was the conference's plenary speaker. He went on to comment that "This group has an important role to play in nurturing practitioners who can provide effective one-on-one therapy while also advocating for and working in partnerships that can achieve real structural change."

Adler School of Professional Psychology

THE ADLER SCHOOL

The Adler School of Professional Psychology (Adler School) was established in 1952 and is a private, not-for-profit institution of higher education. With a commitment to continuing the work of the first community psychologist, Alfred Adler, the Adler School hold the following values as core to our educational programs: social interest, compassion, justice, respect for the individual, honor for diversity and difference, intellectual rigor, optimism, collaboration and pragmatism. The school is an independent school of professional psychology, drawing students from North America and internationally.

Building on the work of Alfred Adler, the vision of the Adler School of Professional Psychology emphasizes the importance of educating socially responsible practitioners. In accordance with Adlerian principles, it is only through interest in the broader community that humans evolve. Adler extended the view to recognize the larger context, including the social conditions, within which individuals are situated.

Adler was among the first to document the impact of social conditions on population health. Adler's first book, more than 100 years ago, described how social factors impact health and well-being. His book demonstrated how poor living and working conditions in 19th century Vienna caused health problems such as respiratory, infectious, and other diseases.

ADLER INSTITUTE ON SOCIAL EXCLUSION

The mission of the Adler Institute on Social Exclusion (ISE) is to advance social justice. We do this by working to integrate the concept of "social exclusion" into U.S. popular and public policy discourse; by helping to contextualize social disadvantage; and by advancing the idea that the point of intervention for addressing social disadvantage is its social, political, and economic context.

Social exclusion refers to the ways individuals and groups are denied access to rights, opportunities, and resources that are commonly available to most people. Adler School's Institute on Social Exclusion is a catalyst for dialogue and action, helping to remove the often unseen barriers that undermine the ability of individuals to participate in mainstream American life.

The ISE is an integral part of the Adler School's educational programming. A central theme in the work of the Institute on Social Exclusion is the idea that social injustice is often created by structural features of society such as laws, public policies, institutional behaviors, and popular ideologies and beliefs. Institute on Social Exclusion's Faculty Fellows, Faculty Affiliates, students, and community partners collaboratively engage in a variety of research, community outreach, and public awareness project.

To learn more about the Adler Institute on Social Exclusion, e-mail ISE@adler.edu.

ADLER INSTITUTE ON PUBLIC SAFETY AND SOCIAL JUSTICE

The mission of the Adler Institute on Public Safety and Social Justice (IPSSJ) is to promote social justice by increasing awareness of socially just policies and practices within the realms of law enforcement and homeland security, and actively working to encourage others to adopt such practices through public dialogue and community involvement.

The Adler Institute on Public Safety and Social Justice's objectives for creating social change includes: community outreach that addresses community-identified social justice issues; public education and awareness to encourage public dialogue around national safety and security and socially just policy issues; and applied research that informs public safety and national security policies and practices. To learn more about the Adler Institute on Public Safety and Social Justice, e-mail IPSSJ@adler.edu.

Social Determinants of Mental Health, Working Definition

The Adler Institute on Social Exclusion has crafted a working definition of the social determinants of mental health that is in accord with the position of the World Health Organization's (WHO) Commission on Social Determinants of Health. The WHO described the social determinants of health as the conditions in which people "are born, grow, live, work and age" and which "are shaped by the distribution of money, power and resources at global, national and local levels" (WHO, 2009). According to the WHO, these conditions are influenced by policy choices and are primarily responsible for disparities in health.

Social determinants of mental health means those elements of social structure most closely shown to affect health and illness, including at a minimum:

Income inequality	Education	Social exclusion
Food security	Literacy	Political disadvantage
Housing quality	Employment conditions	Marginalization
Social status	Discrimination	Health systems
Violence	Cultural norms	Public service systems

Public service systems play especially important roles in shaping the social determinants of health through policies, programs, and resulting resource allocations. Relevant public service systems include those concerned with social welfare, housing, public safety, health care, justice, transportation, and land use/planning. As a result, a social determinants-informed approach to address health disparities focuses on broad scale public systems reform.

The social determinants framework has been widely applied to physical health conditions such as heart disease, cancer, and obesity. Mental health applications have been far fewer, however. The result is a relative lack of attention to how the social determinants identified above can affect mental health. The Institute on Social Exclusion's multidisciplinary team seeks to address this gap through research, outreach, and educational programming that highlights how social conditions impact mental health.

Many communities around the world are plagued by high rates of poverty, joblessness, violence, discrimination, poor-quality housing, and limited access to services. Community members suffer disproportionately from stress, anxiety, trauma, depression, and substance abuse, which in turn can perpetuate many of the original social problems.

Traditional behavioral health prevention and intervention strategies aim to effect change in the suffering individual. The Institute on Social Exclusion's additional focus on the social determinants of mental health, with multiple levels of systems intervention, seeks to address the root causes of the distress that can affect vulnerable and disadvantaged populations.

Keynote Address: David Satcher, M.D., Ph.D.

SUMMARY

The Social Determinants of Mental Health conference commenced with an informative keynote address by Dr. David Satcher, the 16th Surgeon General of the United States, former Director of the CDC, member of the World Health Organization Commission on Social Determinants of Health, and currently the Director of the Satcher Health Leadership Institute at the Morehouse School of Medicine.

Dr. Satcher's presentation promoted an awareness of how the physical and social environments affect mental health. In addition, Dr. Satcher advocated for utilizing community interventions and national strategies, such as creating policy reform, in order to actively intervene and foster interdisciplinary conversations to promote optimal mental health.

Dr. Satcher invited audience members to think critically about the notion of mental health, defined as the "successful performance of mental function, resulting in productive activities, fulfilling relationships with others, and the ability to adapt to change and to cope successfully with adversity."

While prevailing efforts addressed only treatment for mental illness, Dr. Satcher refocused attention upon promoting mental health through detection and prevention. In particular, he suggested that mental health should not be taken for granted because everyone is at risk for mental illness. He advocated that mental health is fundamental for overall health and well-being. Therefore, individuals need to be attuned to their behavior, such as smoking, eating, and exercise, their family's genetic history, their ability to access health care, and their environment because these are determinants that influence one's health.

Dr. Satcher emphasized the need for a global movement of like-minded socially responsible individuals to form alliances to address social determinants of mental

Keynote Address

health. Consistent with the conference's theme "Awareness to Action," Dr. Satcher urged people to rally across the country to encourage politicians to create the policy changes necessary to improve the social determinants of mental health. He explained that "social determinants of health" refers to the "conditions in which people are born, grow, live, work and age". These conditions are "shaped by the distribution of money, power and resources at global, national and local levels".

Dr. Satcher stated that his involvement with the World Health Organization Commission on Social Determinants of Health was only the initial step in "fostering a global movement that places fair health – fairer distribution of health and better overall population health – at the head and the heart of governance". In essence, changes to social determinants of health can occur, but often require policy changes.

To demonstrate the importance of promoting preventative mental health, Dr. Satcher discussed children as an exemplar population in which early interventions have been shown to affect health outcomes. He explained that, during childhood and adolescence, mental health is defined as: the achievement of expected developmental cognitive, social and emotional milestones; secure attachments; satisfying social relationships and effective coping skills.

Dr. Satcher asserted that mentally healthy children enjoy a positive quality of life, function well at school, at home, and in their communities. They are also free of disabling symptoms of psychopathology. Dr. Satcher suggested that there are many social determinants impeding children's ability to develop healthy, including: poverty, unsatisfying relationships with caregivers, exposure to traumatic events, and prenatal exposure to toxins.

Dr. Satcher recommended several preventative interventions, like educational programs for young children, parent education programs, and collaboration between primary care providers and schools. This interdisciplinary, multi-setting, systemic network highlights the community's responsibility, in addition to the individual's responsibility, for sustaining one's mental health and establishing a vibrant community.

Furthermore, Dr. Satcher argued that this approach could improve children's eating habits by increasing access to nutritious foods, increasing children's physical activity, and educating teachers and parents about the benefits of proper nutrition and physical activity on academic performance and physical and mental health.

Dr. Satcher recommended "Mental Health: A Report of the Surgeon General" (1999) and its supplement "Mental Health: Culture, Race, and Ethnicity (2001)" because both documents introduced the concept of mental health to the American public. In essence, Dr. Satcher advocated that culture does interact with the social determinants of mental health, and therefore needs to be understood and addressed. Dr. Satcher suggested that culture affects how the client manifests and describes mental illness, how one copes with mental illness, what type of stressors one experiences, and whether or not one is willing to seek mental health services.

Additionally, Dr. Satcher stated that culture also impacts health care professionals in their ability to diagnose clients, offer various types of treatment, and organize and finance services. Dr. Satcher noted that stigma of mental illness is still a deterrent to mental health treatment in many communities. Stigma prevents individuals from acknowledging mental health concerns. Stigma also prevents individuals from requesting help for family and friends. Stigma also prevents the government and the private sector from addressing structural challenges when addressing mental health treatment.

Consistent with his role as the "Doctor of the Nation," Dr. Satcher concluded his presentation by prescribing some health recommendations to improve the well-being of individuals and communities. His recommendations included: pursuing moderate physical activity (at least 5 days a week, 30 minutes per day); eating at least 5 serving of fruits and vegetables a day; avoiding toxins (e.g. tobacco, illicit drugs, alcohol abuse); engaging in responsible sexual behavior; and participating daily in relaxing and stress reducing activities. Dr. Satcher firmly believes it is the integration of personal, family, and social responsibility that results in good mental health.

During the question and answer period, one participant suggested that there is a need to have a broad based reform in the United States to allow policy makers to have conversations about income redistribution without being blamed for socialistic thought. Dr. Satcher's request to form alliances, and recognize what other disciplines can offer to the mental health arena resonated with many participants.

Dr. Satcher suggested that creating trans-disciplinary collaborations requires individuals to spend time developing their common goals and forming a meaningful relationship. Dr. Satcher challenged all individuals to consider that all policy is health policy. In turn, when evaluating a policy in a community, one needs to be astute to recognize its potential health impact. Many participants commended Dr.

Satcher for his leadership and his ability to translate health awareness into meaningful information that policy makers and the American public may use to affect decision-making.

BIOGRAPHY

David Satcher, MD, PhD is Director of The Satcher Health Leadership Institute which was established in 2006 at the Morehouse School of Medicine in Atlanta, Georgia. The mission of the Institute is to develop a diverse group of public health leaders, foster and support leadership strategies, and influence policies toward the reduction and ultimate elimination of disparities in health. The Institute's programs reflect Dr. Satcher's experience in improving public health policy and his commitment to eliminating health disparities for underserved groups, such as minorities and the poor and shedding light on neglected issues, such as mental and sexual health.

Dr. Satcher was sworn in as the 16th Surgeon General of the United States in 1998. He also served as Assistant Secretary for Health in the Department of Health and Human Services from February 1998 to January 2001, making him only the second person in history to have held both positions simultaneously. He was the first person to have served as Director of the CDC and then Surgeon General of the United States.

He also presently occupies the Poussaint-Satcher-Cosby Chair in Mental Health at the Morehouse School of Medicine. This recognizes his long commitment to removing the stigma attached to mental illness, as evidenced by Mental Health: A Report of the Surgeon, the first surgeon general's report on mental health released during his tenure as surgeon general.

As Surgeon General and Assistant Secretary for Health, Dr. Satcher led the department's effort to eliminate racial and ethnic disparities in health, an initiative that was incorporated as one of the two major goals of Healthy People 2010. Dr. Satcher held the position of Director of the National Center for Primary Care (NCPC) at the Morehouse School of Medicine from 2002 to 2004.

Dr. Satcher has received over 40 honorary degrees and numerous distinguished honors including top awards from the National Medical Association, the American Medical Association, the American Academy of Family Physicians and the Symbol of H.O.P.E. Award for health promotion and disease prevention. In 2005, he was appointed to serve on the World Health Organization Commission on Social Determinants of Health.

Dr. Satcher graduated from Morehouse College in Atlanta, Georgia. He holds MD and PhD degrees from Case Western Reserve University in Ohio. He is a member of Alpha Omega Alpha Honor Society and a Fellow of the American Academy of Family Physicians, the American College of Preventive Medicine and the American College of Physicians. In addition, he is a member of the Institute of Medicine, National Academy of Sciences, the 100 Black Men of Atlanta and the American Academy of Arts and Sciences.

PANEL DISCUSSION SUMMARY

Following Dr. David Satcher's keynote address, a discussion commenced with a panel of experts who have made outstanding contributions to public health, community health, and medicine.

Dr. Marian McDonald, Associate Director of Health Disparities, National Center for Emerging and Zoonotic Infectious Diseases at the Centers for Disease Control and Prevention, served as moderator. Dr. McDonald asserted that the aim of the panel conversation was to respond to Dr. Satcher and apply his insights to various fields to advance the American public's understanding of the Social Determinants of Mental Health framework.

In particular, the panel aimed to advance development by discussing how Social Determinants of Mental Health framework can be operationalized in the mental health arena and by highlighting the benefits and challenges of incorporating this framework into the health care delivery system.

Dr. Terry Mason, the Chief Medical Officer of the Cook County Health System (Metropolitan Chicago), initiated the panel discussion. Dr. Mason addressed the "health care myth" by positing that our current medical practices focus on disease detection and treatment, rather than on health promotion. He attempted to eliminate the confusing distinction between the notion of early modality detection and that of true prevention.

Dr. Mason used the Adverse Child Experience (ACE) study, as an example to underscore that mental illness is preventable. This research linked childhood environment impact on health behavior. The study demonstrated that there is a direct correlation between events, such as physical/emotional/sexual abuse, parental drug

use, and family chronic mental illness, with health behavior like smoking, drinking, having multiple sex partners, and using IV drugs among middle-class educated white participants in California.

Dr. Mason further suggested that individuals, who make poor health choices, subsequently have disease, disability, and myriad social problems. Dr. Mason stated that there needs to be a change in the perception of what the current health care system does and how it is financed. Currently, the American public needs to understand there is a disease detection and management system in which practitioners do not cure, but instead manage symptoms. In the future, Dr. Mason suggested that further efforts should to be concentrated on prevention and health promotion.

Dr. Gail Christopher, Vice President for Programs, Food, Health, and Well-Being at the W.K. Kellogg Foundation, commented on the application of the Social Determinants framework and its application to the mental health field. She discussed how the W.K. Kellogg Foundation's vision is a nation that marshals its resources to ensure all children thrive and to create conditions that propel vulnerable children to succeed.

Subsequently, Dr. Christopher noted that W.K. Kellogg Foundation has developed a strategy of healing remnants of racism and identifying structural racism to improve mental well-being. Consistent with the conference's theme of "Awareness to Action," Dr. Christopher observed that society should address the legacy of a belief system that excludes individuals based on perceived differences. That, she argued, would be an effective way to address the Social Determinants of Mental Health. Furthermore, she pointed out the need to invest in communities that are willing to strive to eradicate racism. Doing so, Dr. Christopher suggested, would lead to establishing communities with psyches free of racism.

Dr. Aida Giachello, Director of the Midwest Latino Health Research, Training and Policy Center at the University of Illinois at Chicago, discussed the importance of personal and social responsibility. Her research found that psychosocial experiences in the work environment are linked to poor health outcomes like depression and alcohol usage among minority individuals.

Dr. Giachello advocated that it is important for practitioners to understand the dynamics of providing mental health services to minorities. She highlighted that both finances and linguistics are major barriers that minorities face when attempting to access mental health services. She proposed a recipe for cultural competency in organizations that included expansion of diversity in key leadership roles to shape organizational norms and practices; allocation of finances to reflect a value of cultural sensitivity; development of organizational policies to ensure sliding scales and improvement of entry into services.

Dr. Giachello suggested that an ecological model could encourage individual's propensity to move from awareness to action by establishing interdisciplinary partnerships. Dr. Giachello observed that a model, like one adopted in Brazil, may further our understanding of the importance of Social Determinants of Mental Health. She reported that the constitution in Brazil includes health as a fundamental right. At the government level, inter-departmental partnerships are formed and health policy is considered in all portfolios of government – e.g., economy, housing, and education. In addition to the Ministry of Health, all of Brazil's government is committed to consider ways to improve health and quality of life within the country.

Dr. Giachello recommended that partnerships should be formed within the United States to advance human capital, organize and empower individuals, and improve our environment so that our society's mental well-being will be enriched.

The panel discussion concluded with Dr. Aaron Wernham, Director of the Health Impact Project at the Pew Health Group, Pew Charitable Trusts, who addressed the genesis of Health Impact Assessment (HIA). Dr. Wernham explained that a Health Impact Assessment is an effective tool to transition from awareness of Social Determinants of Mental Health to provide action recommendations.

Dr. Wernham advocated that individual health is more than just the combination of genetics and behavior, since it must also take into account the context of the individual. For example, a diabetic individual may take his insulin. However, he or she may be prevented from exercising or taking a walk outside because he or she lives in an unsafe neighborhood. Dr. Wernham affirmed, "We need to think about creating the conditions in communities that allow people to reach their potential to be healthy." He suggested, "the conditions in communities really result from a specific set of decisions that are made across a myriad of other sectors, most of which never consider the health implications."

Subsequently, Dr. Wernham noted that it is the responsibility of practitioners, researchers, and mental health professionals to invite health professionals to public decision-making forums, and that the health impact assessment is one mechanism to attract them. He reminded conference attendees that decisions about the health

and well-being of the community are made daily by the government. The government needs to consider the health impact of these decisions before formulating legislation and public policy. Equipped with a Health Impact Assessment, health advocates can be agents of change by informing key decision makers of recommendations for optimal health outcomes. He suggested that, by planning ahead, the government can consider what the potential health impacts are and how the community will manage them.

Dr. Wernham explained that the Health Impact Assessment is a systematic and participatory approach that brings together public health science and data, along with community input to synthesize a picture of the potential impacts. Dr. Wernham emphasized that Health Impact Assessment is a structured approach for public health professionals to enter into a dialogue with persons from other sectors – e.g., city planners, transportation officials, education departments, departments of agriculture, government, and environmental planning agencies -- and to engage those individuals in meaningful conversation to advocate for mental health. Since it considers health, even when a decision does not appear to be about health, the Health Impact Assessment makes health a priority in the decision making process.

Dr. Wernham explained that health professionals need to be encouraged to attend forums to collaborate with health professionals and members of other sectors to ensure that mental health is included in the decision-making process.

PANELIST BIOGRAPHIES

Gail C. Christopher, D.N.

Vice President for Programs, Food, Health and Well-Being, W.K. Kellogg Foundation

Dr. Christopher is vice president for programs at the W.K. Kellogg Foundation in Battle Creek, Michigan. In this role, she serves on the executive team that provides overall direction and leadership for the Kellogg Foundation and provides leadership for Food, Health & Well-Being, and Racial Equity programming. She is a nationally recognized leader in health policy, with particular expertise and experience in the issues related to social determinants of health, health disparities and public policy issues of concern to African Americans and other minority populations. A prolific writer and presenter, she is the author or co-author of three books, a monthly column in the Federal Times, and more than 250 articles, presentations, and publications. Prior to joining the Kellogg Foundation, Dr. Christopher was vice president of the Joint Center for Political and Economic Studies' Office of Health, Women and Families in Washington, D.C. She holds a doctor of naprapathy degree from the Chicago National College of Naprapathy in Illinois and completed advanced study in the interdisciplinary Ph.D. program in holistic health and clinical nutrition at the Union for Experimenting Colleges and Universities at Union Graduate School of Cincinnati, Ohio.

Aida Giachello, Ph.D.

Director, Midwest Latino Health Research, Training & Policy Center, University of Illinois at Chicago

Dr. Aida Giachello is an associate professor in the Jane Addams College of Social Work at the University of Illinois at Chicago and has been director of the College's Midwest Latino Health Research, Training and Policy Center since it was founded in 1993. The Midwest Latino Center follows community participatory action research and empowerment models that use research for community mobilization and action to address social justice issues. In 2005, Dr. Giachello was named in TIME Magazine as one of twenty-five most influential Hispanic/Latino persons in America. Dr. Giachello has her master's degree in social services administration and a PhD in Medical Sociology, specializing in Hispanic/Latino minority health from the University of Chicago. In addition to her research background, Dr. Giachello is a community organizer and an agent of social change, advocating on behalf of racial and ethnic minorities, women as a group, and the poor and elderly.

Terry Mason, M.D.

Chief Medical Officer, Cook County Health System (Metropolitan Chicago)

Dr. Mason currently serves as the Chief Medical Officer of the Cook County Health and Hospitals Systems (CCHHS). Previously, he was the Commissioner of the Chicago Department of Public Health. Dr. Mason is and has been a strong advocate in changing the health landscape to our cities by bringing more healthy food choices into all neighborhoods. More recently, he has been the public face of the city and Cook County's fight to educate and prepare the public for the H1N1 novel influenza outbreak. He is a board certified Urologist who has enjoyed a 25 year career in medical practice. He received his medical degree from the University of Illinois, Abraham Lincoln School of Medicine in Chicago, is Board Certified by the American Board of Urology, is a Fellow at the American College of Surgeons and is a past member of the Executive Committee of the Chicago Urological Association. Dr. Mason has long been a nationally known health educator and inspirational speaker. He champions holistic approaches to health management, the role of families in building healthier communities and the elimination of racial and ethnic disparities in health.

Aaron Wernham, M.D.

Director, Health Impact Project, Pew Health Group, The Pew Charitable Trusts

Dr. Wernham is the Director of the Health Impact Project, a collaboration of the Robert Wood Johnson Foundation and The Pew Charitable Trusts, designed to promote the use of health impact assessments (HIAs) and support the growth of the field in the United States. He is an HIA expert who has led HIAs at the state and federal levels, has conducted HIA trainings for, collaborated with, and advised numerous health and environmental regulatory agencies, on integrating HIAs into their programs. Prior to joining Pew, Dr. Wernham was a senior policy analyst with the Alaska Native Tribal Health Consortium, where he led the first successful efforts in the United States to formally integrate HIAs into the federal environmental impact statement process. Dr. Wernham received his medical degree from the University of California, San Francisco, a master's degree in health and medical sciences from the University of California, Berkeley, and is board certified in family medicine.

Panel Discussion

Marian McDonald, Dr.P.H., M.P.H., M.A. (Moderator)

Associate Director of Health Disparities, National Center for Emerging and Zoonotic Infectious Diseases, Centers for Disease Control and Prevention

Dr. McDonald joined CDC in 2002 as Associate Director for Minority & Women's Health for the National Center for Infectious Diseases (now the National Center for Emerging and Zoonotic Infectious Diseases). Dr. McDonald has worked in minority health and women's health for three decades as an educator, scientist, and advocate. She received her DrPH and MPH from the University of California at Berkeley School of Public Health, and holds a Masters in Women's Studies from Goddard College. Formerly a professor at Tulane University School of Public Health, her expertise includes cultural competence in public health and social determinants of infectious diseases. At CDC, Dr. McDonald spearheaded and chaired the first International Conference on Women and Infectious Diseases (ICWID), held in Atlanta February 2004. She has been part of the leadership of CDC's efforts on Neglected Infections of Poverty. Dr. McDonald has worked extensively in Latino health, founding the Latino Health Outreach Project, the Latino Children's Health Network, and the Hispanic Women's Health Group in New Orleans. She has received numerous awards and honors for her contributions to health equity.

The Adler Institute on Social Exclusion

Plenary Presentation: Sandro Galea, M.D., M.P.H., Dr.P.H.

SUMMARY

The second day of the Social Determinants of Mental Health conference commenced with an informative plenary address by Dr. Sandro Galea, Gelman Professor and Chair of the Department of Epidemiology at Columbia University's Mailman School of Public Health.

Drawing from his professional expertise as a physician and epidemiologist, Dr. Galea promoted an awareness of the Social Determinants of Population Mental Health by discussing the intersection of social epidemiology and population health.

In particular, Dr. Galea summarized the evidence that supports the notion that social factors, like individual, interpersonal and ecological, influence mental health. Additionally, Dr. Galea advocated that the mental health field needs to appreciate the social determinants framework in order to further advance the field.

Dr. Galea challenged audience members to consider how social determinants influence mental health. He defined social determinants as exogenous factors which impact health. Dr. Galea emphasized that the health field must come to the understanding that external social factors affect one's internal processes and, in turn, one's physical and mental health. Evidence has demonstrated that external factors influence internal factors of health, such as intuition, and geographic health disparities as well.

Dr. Galea argued that society's intuition about public health is that the environment in which one is embedded influences one's level of health. In addition, there is a need to understand better how exogenous mechanisms relate to endogenous factors. For example, genetic factors cannot solely explain the health disparities that occur across the United States.

Dr. Galea addressed the genesis of the Social Determinants of Health framework. He explained that publications, from as far back as 1939, contained several studies suggesting higher prevalence of mental illness in inner-city neighborhoods than suburban communities do. He suggested there is early evidence to support how social environment – e.g., urban living conditions and types of occupations -- impacts mental health.

To date, there continues to be a growing body of evidence to support Social Determinants of Mental Health, in terms of external characteristics of people, their relationship to others, and their experience in a built environment. For example, Dr. Galea noted that low socioeconomic status is associated with mental illness, especially mood and anxiety disorders. Also, individuals, who witness violence in their neighborhoods, have a higher prevalence of mental illness. Dr. Galea explained that social support continues to be a vital driver of mental health. Furthermore, Dr. Galea observed that there exists research showing a link between ecological factors, like the built environment and the economy, and the prevalence of mental illness.

In the public health field, there is an understanding that social environment influences mental health. Dr. Galea commented that three challenges need to be addressed to increase awareness and advance the Social Determinants framework. These challenges include methods, constructs and concepts.

In terms of methods, there remains a limited understanding of whether social factors are associated with mental health, or vice versa, since many studies are cross-sectional. In addition, studies that have poorly specified causal models are ones that do not properly address confounding variables. Dr. Galea reported that longitudinal research has been used recently as one attempt to clarify this issue.

The second challenge for proponents of the Social Determinants of Health framework is addressing and operationalizing constructs. It is difficult to link social determinants because the meanings of mental health terms are often muddled.

Furthermore, there are fundamental problems that underlie the conceptualization of Social Determinants of Health. For example, one has difficulty observing social determinants when utilizing only a small restricted sample. One will not be able to see all of the associations unless a larger sample, which exposes the sample's heterogeneity, is used.

Dr. Galea proposed two recommendations to address the challenges that confront the Social Determinants of Health framework. First, he recommended drawing on social epidemiology, which explicitly studies exposures, as an approach to organizing pertinent information. Second, he recommended learning from the field of population health.

Dr. Galea emphasized the importance of focusing our attention on the causes and burdens of diseases for the entire populations, and not limiting our understanding merely to the level of individuals. For example, macro-social forces, like the economy and urbanization, can affect the population's distribution of mental health over the next decade. This understanding can improve the collective health and well-being of the population.

Consistent with the conference's theme "Awareness to Action," Dr. Galea advocated that there are four challenges that the Social Determinants of Mental Health community should tackle. First, he identified the need to understand the influence of macro-social forces on population mental health. Second, he suggested using a population health framework to reduce the prevalence of mental illness within populations. Next, Dr. Galea acknowledged that both social and biological factors matter when dealing with mental health. Finally, he recommended adopting innovative methods to overcome the challenges presented by the relevant literature.

Dr. Galea concluded his presentation by summarizing the current intersection of Public Health, Epidemiology, and Social Determinants of Mental Health. Dr. Galea stated that it is vital to understand the social roots of mental illness. He indicated that a recent drift toward molecular causes have dampened scientific progress about Social Determinants of Mental Health. Several methodological and conceptual barriers have contributed to the limited pace of adopting the Social Determinants framework in the mental health field.

In addition, Dr. Galea affirmed that to advance the field, the mental health community should place Social Determinants of Mental Health in the center of inquiry. Doing that will have the effect of increasing our understanding of how both social and biological factors influence mental health.

During the question and answer session, Dr. Galea stated, "In the context of a school of practitioners, you have a powerful pedagogical tool which is the fact that you are dealing with real people and real patients. I think that it's immensely powerful and instructive in educating those around you about what needs to be done to shift the curve of mental health. I think an institution, like the Adler School, could be quite powerful in pushing on policies and integration of our thinking around these areas and leading the way forward."

BIOGRAPHY

Sandro Galea, MD, DrPH, is the Gelman Professor and Chair of the Department of Epidemiology at Columbia University's Mailman School of Public Health. He is a physician and an epidemiologist. His primary research has been on the causes of mental disorders, particularly common mood-anxiety disorders and substance abuse, and on the role of traumatic events in shaping population health. In particular, his work seeks to uncover how determinants at multiple levels of influence--including policies, features of the social environment, molecular, and genetic factors--jointly produce the health of urban populations.

Dr. Galea has conducted large population-based studies in several countries worldwide including the US, Spain, Israel, Ethiopia, Tanzania, and Liberia, primarily funded by the National Institutes of Health. Dr Galea's interest in the complex etiology of health and disease has led him to work that explores innovative methodological approaches to population health questions primarily funded by a Robert Wood Johnson Health Policy Investigator Award.

Dr Galea has published more than 250 scientific journal articles, 50 chapters and commentaries, and five books. Prior to his arrival at Columbia's Mailman School of Public Health, Dr Galea was on faculty at the University of Michigan. Dr. Galea's work has been featured in such media outlets as The New York Times, NPR, and NBC. He was named one of TIME magazine's epidemiology innovators in 2006.

Dr. Galea completed his Medical Degree at the University of Toronto, a Masters of Public Health from Harvard University, and a Doctorate in Public Health from Columbia University. He has received multiple honors and awards including: the McMaster University; Peter J. Neelands Invitational Lectureship award, New York Academy of Medicine; elected Fellow, the Columbia University Mailman School of Public Health; William Farr Award in Epidemiology, the Robert Wood Johnson Foundation Health Policy Investigator Award, and the John C Cassel Memorial Lecture; Society for Epidemiologic Research.

Concurrent Session 1: Awareness

1.1: ECONOMIC CONDITIONS AS SOCIAL DETERMINANTS
Presenters: Denise M. Zabkiewicz, PhD; Kara Zivin, PhD

SUMMARY

Previous research establishes a robust relationship between economic conditions and mental health. Employment promotes mental well-being, potentially because it increases social support, self-esteem or mastery, and financial security. Our speakers, however, discussed how this finding does not always hold equally for all persons.

Dr. Zabkiewicz emphasized the importance of context when applying research findings to applied settings. For example, poor women constitute a unique population; they are typically single, have less education, have fewer job opportunities, and often hold unstable, temporary jobs, which rarely offer employment benefits. The relationship between employment and mental health outcomes, however, is not well known for poor women.

To explore this knowledge gap, Dr. Zabkiewicz investigated employment, family structure, and depression in this population to address two questions: 1) Is current unemployment among poor US women associated with reduced depression? and 2) Does the relationship between employment and depression vary by family context?

Using data from the 2000 National Alcohol Survey, Dr. Zabkiewicz found that overall depression rates were significantly lower among employed women; however, the beneficial impact of employment did not vary by part-time or full-time status. Interestingly, depression rates varied as a function of family demands; thus, only women with low family demands experienced the benefits of employment with respect to depression. More specifically, for those with high family demands (defined as three or more children), depression rates were equal regardless of employment status. In other words, there was no expected reduction in depression among employed women. However, employed women with smaller families (two or fewer children) had lower rates of depression relative to unemployed women. Specifically, these women experienced half the rate of depression relative to their unemployed counterparts. Although the underlying mechanism for the development of depression within this context is unknown, these results suggest that some women are disproportionately economically and emotionally vulnerable.

Although employment is an important protective factor against depression, women may not always reap its benefits. In other words, "work does not work for all women." Reasons for this include the five-year limit for welfare aid, lack of affordable childcare options, and welfare vouchers that are insufficient, temporary, and difficult to obtain in a timely manner. In contrast, the interaction of economics and employment do not yield the same trends for middle class women. This could be due to the likelihood that this subpopulation has more flexible jobs, better access to healthcare, and more financial resources that serve as protective factors.

Similarly, Dr. Kara Zivin investigated the impact of economic recessions on mental health by conducting a critical systematic review of published literature ranging from the 19th century until the 1980's. Previous research (i.e., Durkheim, Brenner) suggested that the economic climate greatly influences psychological distress and mental hospitalization rates. Zivin's study emphasized population health indicators to address the psychological implications of macroeconomic policy decisions. Based on the results of this review, her study examined three primary mental health indicators: 1) mental disorders, 2) admissions to mental health facilities, and 3) suicide.

The study found that economic downturns correlated with increased psychological distress, particularly in vulnerable subgroups of the general population. For example, those in the workforce during a recession and/or in a lower socioeconomic group with less education were more negatively affected than those who were already unemployed or in a higher status group. Further, during an economic crisis, overall rates of mental health facility use and suicide rates increase significantly, reflecting greater psychological distress.

Although these indicators may vary across gender, age, and occupational status, the overall trend remains stable over geographical locations, methodologies, and time. One possible explanation for these findings is the Shift Hypothesis, which states that unemployment causes the loss of insurance resulting in increased use of the public health system and limited access to other healthcare and resources. This study also suggests that increased social support and protection during economic declines may mitigate negative impacts upon mental health and thereby prevent unemployment, suicide, and usage of mental health facilities. Future research should target social programs that may decrease psychological distress during periods of economic decline.

Following the presentations, the audience and speakers generated ideas for preventative strategies to ameliorate the emotional repercussions of recession. For example, increasing childcare options to eliminate barriers to employment was viewed as a priority. It was also emphasized that prevention services should be tied to the labor market through health insurance.

On a population level, universal healthcare systems as seen in Scandinavian countries may mitigate the detrimental effects of economic downturns. Taken together, the work by Drs. Zabkiewicz and Zivin is timely and relevant given the current economic situation in the 21st century, and it underscores the importance of economic decline as a social determinant of mental health.

SESSION 1.1 ABSTRACTS

Employment and Depression Among US Women Living in Poverty

Denise M. Zabkiewicz, PhD

Center for Applied Research in Mental Health and Addictions Faculty of Health Sciences, Simon Fraser University, Burnaby, Canada. Co-authors: Laura A. Schmidt, PhD; James Wiley, PhD

The relationship between employment and improved mental health is well documented. However, no research has examined whether this relationship applies to poor women. For women living in poverty, the competing demands of work and childcare may operate to prevent them from reaping the mental health benefits of employment. Understanding these connections has become more salient not just for mental health epidemiology but for policies targeting employment and poverty. This study draws on the NIH-funded 2000 National Alcohol Survey (NAS) amongst a nationally representative sample of U.S. adults. For purposes of this analysis, the sample was restricted to the 658 poor women who participated in the NAS.

Multivariate logistic regression models assessed the relationship between employment and depression as well as the moderating role of family demands. Overall, the findings are consistent with the long-standing literature surrounding the mental health benefits of work. Here, current employment was associated with reduced rates of depression.

However, the results were found to vary by family demands. For poor women with heavy child-rearing responsibilities, employment was not associated with reduced rates of depression. Only employed women with a moderate level of family demands experienced lower rates of depression. Although prior research has documented the mental health benefits of employment, researchers have often failed to account for the economic and family contexts of working women.

While the findings of this study support the robust relationship between employment and mental health, they also suggest that family environments may be a precondition for poor women to reap the mental health benefits of work.

In the current context of economic decline coupled with widespread welfare reform, the findings of this study have far-reaching implications for welfare policy as they provide an important and timely perspective in our understanding of the relationship between employment and mental health among poor women.

Economic Downturns and Population Mental Health: A Systemic Review

Kara Zivin, PhD

Department of Psychiatry, University of Michigan, Department of Veterans Affairs, National Serious Mental Illness Treatment Research and Evaluation Center, Ann Arbor MI. Co-authors: Magdalena Paczkowski, MPH; Sandro Galea, MD, DrPH

Prior research suggests that the current global economic crisis may be negatively affecting population mental health. We sought to conduct a systematic synthesis of the literature using PRISMA guidelines on the relation between economic recessions and population mental health.

We searched MEDLINE and PsychINFO databases using key words related to mental health and economic crisis. We included articles that used the unemployment rate as its macroeconomic indicator and longitudinal data analysis methods. We identified additional articles from citations of articles we found via our search.

We did not limit our search to any particular geographic region or time period. We did not examine the relationship between an individual's employment status and psychiatric diagnosis, and we excluded review articles, books or book chapters, and studies focused on children or adolescents.

For each study included we noted the geographic location, time period, frequency of measurement, economic and mental health indicators, statistical method(s) used, and main findings. Sixty-two articles met our study criteria. They included analyses of economic trends dating back to 1870, and examined worldwide population mental health data.

We identified three primary mental health indicators: mental disorders, admissions to mental health facilities, and suicide. The substantial majority of articles found a significant association between economic downturns and increased prevalence and severity of mental disorders, frequency of admissions to mental health facilities, and rates of suicide.

Economic crises are negatively associated with population mental health. How economic downturns influence mental health should be considered in policies that aim to promote recovery.

1.2: SOCIAL DETERMINANTS OF SUICIDE
Presenters: Samantha L. Matlin, PhD; Valerie Borum, PhD, MSW

SUMMARY

During the awareness-themed session entitled the "Social Determinants of Suicide" both Dr. Samantha Matlin and Dr. Valerie Borum presented their respective research pertaining to suicide within specific minority groups.

Dr. Matlin discussed the Social Determinants of Suicidal Behaviors among African American and Hispanic Adolescents. She addressed an increase in the incidence of suicide in minority groups (e.g., African Americans and Hispanic / Latinos) who have traditionally had lower rates of suicide. Dr. Matlin noted that, despite this increase in minority populations, Caucasian Americans continue to be the subjects of most research in suicide.

Dr. Matlin observed that, while depression is a risk factor for suicide in adolescents, social support serves as a potential protective factor for suicide behavior. The concept of social support was framed using the term connectedness. Connectedness occurs between individuals, individuals and their families to community organizations, and among community organizations and social institutions.

Factors that impede neighborhood cohesiveness include high residential mobility and concentration of low socioeconomic families in small spaces. This is particularly poignant when one acknowledges that both African American and Hispanic adolescents live in neighborhoods with higher levels of concentrated disadvantage. She acknowledged that the Social Determinants of Health at different ecological levels include child health, parent and family health, community health, and social services systems.

Dr. Matlin discussed her present study that focuses on African American and Hispanic youth, as well as the risk and protective factors for suicide ideation and attempts across multiple ecological levels. In-home interviews with children and adolescents between the ages of 11-18 years took place between April and December 1995. That study supported the hypothesis that adult social support seems to play an important role in risks associated with suicide.

In keeping with the conference's awareness theme, Dr. Borum discussed Perceptions of Suicide Risk and Support Among African American College Students: An Afro-centric Theoretical Framework. In addressing the significance of suicide as a problem among African Americans, she noted that on an average day in the United States, approximately one African American dies because of suicide every 4.5 hours. Suicide is the fourth leading cause of death for youth between 10-14 years of age. Reportedly, African American rates of suicide have increased rapidly such that when one disaggregates by race, African Americans commit suicide at a rate of 5.3 per 100,000. Available research, however, may miscalculate the incidence of suicide among African Americans.

To determine the significance of culturally determined perceptions of suicide, Dr. Borum commented that one only needs to look at how three groups describe suicide. These groups include American-Western culture, which views suicide as an "individual act," various Asian cultures, which view suicide in terms of a system of interpersonal relationships, and African American culture, which sees suicide in a socio-cultural context.

In an effort to understand both the nature and incidence of contemporary suicide within the African American culture, Dr. Borum indicates that research should focus on the historical, socio-cultural, and political features of the African American experience. She also notes the need to comprehend what social determinant has shifted to create the growing incidence of suicide. Dr. Borum's exploratory study involved obtaining information about perceptions of suicide and perceptions of the availability and accessibility of support systems. She utilized focus groups to help uncover the participants' perspective on suicide. From these interactions, she was able to generate knowledge in the form of lay theories based on the research participants' understanding of concepts associated with suicide.

Researchers collected data from 38 African American participants, who were full time university students and ranged from 18 to 39 years of age. Dr. Borum reported that participants in all focus groups described their views of suicide in the context of their ethnic cultures and experiences. The main themes that emerged from the discussions were (1) perceptions of suicide, (2) stigma, (3) Black identity, and (4) ownership of life to God.

Attendees asked several questions during the question and answer period. Responding to a question about the incorporation of Emile Durkheim into her theoretical background, Dr. Matlin noted that she focused chiefly on connectedness within the community. Dr. Borum spoke of the importance of developing an Afrocentric theoretical framework in which the African Americans occupy the center of the structure. Dr. Borum went on to suggest that this need to develop a culturally congruent framework for African Americans is necessary to avoid finding patholo-gy, which may indeed merely be a protective factor.

Dr. Matlin also reported that the dataset that she was using also incorporated sex-ual orientation. Finally, Dr. Matlin acknowledged her shared surprise with an au-dience member about her finding that school connectedness was not predictive of reducing the likelihood of suicidal ideations and attempts.

SESSION 1.2 ABSTRACTS

Social Determinants of Suicidal Behaviors among African American and Hispanic Adolescents

Samantha L. Matlin, PhD

The Consultation Center, Yale University School of Medicine, New Haven, CT

Rates of suicide are increasing among racial and ethnic minority youth, including racial/ethnic minority adoles-cents, and pose a significant public health concern. Limited attention has focused on the impact of neighbor-hood and community conditions on suicidal behaviors. Further, research to date has not examined the relative influence of risk and protective factors across various ecological levels (individual, family, peer, and neighbor-hood/community) on suicidal behaviors among adolescents.

This study will utilize a multilevel framework for the study of health behaviors which integrates social and behavioral sciences. Specifically, structural (i.e., poverty, crime), social (i.e., segregation, racism, social position), and behavioral determinants (i.e., depression, stress) of suicidal behaviors will be examined across three eco-logical levels (micro, meso, and macro) among African American and Latino/Hispanic adolescents through the use of a nationally representative dataset – the National Longitudinal Study of Adolescent Health (Add Health).

Data will be used from the in-home adolescent questionnaire, with corresponding data from the in-school ques-tionnaire, parent questionnaire, and community-level indicators (with secondary data measured at the levels of census block group up to county). The proposal will focus on African American (n = 4,807) and Hispanic/Latino (3,525) adolescents aged 13 - 18 years old.

This study increases understanding of how social conditions impact mental health by applying the social determinants frame to suicidal behaviors. This study will create new knowledge with practical applications by identifying risk and protective factors (including mechanisms and pathways by which social context impacts mental health) at multiple ecological levels. These will inform the development of targeted prevention and intervention programs aimed to prevent suicidal behaviors, as well as promote emotional well-being, among racial and ethnic minority youth.

Increased understanding of risk and protection at multiple levels among adolescents is crucial to the develop-ment of culturally competent prevention and intervention programs that can effectively reduce the number of adolescents who die from suicide each year.

Perceptions of Suicide Risk and Support Among African American College Students

Valerie Borum, PhD, MSW

University of Illinois at Chicago, Jane Addams College of Social Work, Chicago, IL

The major objectives of this pilot study were to: 1) explore with a purposive sample of 40 African American college students how ethnic culture impacts perceptions of suicide; and 2) investigate how availability and accessibility of perceived support and other protective factors impact perceptions of suicide.

A Supplement to the Surgeon General's first report, Mental Health: Culture, Race, and Ethnicity (2001), the Surgeon General called for an in-depth understanding and appreciation of how culture influences the nature of suicide and mental illness in ethnically diverse groups. Kiev states that "culture determines the nature of the precipitating factors which trigger off suicidal behavior" (1979, p. 220).

Culture also influences culture-specific choices of method and lethality in suicide (e.g., gun, overdose, hanging, etc.). Suicide is estimated to be the third leading cause of death among persons 15-25 years of age. The suicide rate among African American adolescents (15-19 year-old) increased by 126% between 1980 and 2003 and among youth (10-14 years of age) by 230%, the fourth leading cause of death. African American males account for significant increases.

A total of five focus groups (n=8 each group) were conducted with 38 full-time, African American students enrolled in a large, private university in the northeastern United States for 60-90 minutes each regarding perceptions of suicide and suicide risk and support. Mean age for the total sample 26, with ages ranging from 18 to 39 years.

Focus group findings revealed the following major themes related to perceptions of suicide, risk and support: the influence of the socio-cultural context and social conditions influence perceptions; stigma among family, community, church, and larger society (micro, meso, and macro); Black/African American identity; and the role of the church (e.g., God).

1.3: SOCIAL DETERMINANTS OF CHILDHOOD DEVELOPMENT
**Presenters: Kenneth S. Thompson, MD; Stefania Maggi, PhD;
Nataka Moore, PhD**

SUMMARY

Dr. Kenneth Thompson, Dr. Stefania Maggi, and Dr. Nataka Moore presented at the Social Determinants of Childhood Development session. They agree that children's mental health outcomes are susceptible to the trajectory determined by the community in which they are embedded.

Dr. Thompson, a psychiatrist for the US Department of Health and Human Services, discussed Prevention of Mental Disorders and Substance Abuse among Children, Youth, and Young Adults. He invited participants to consider expanding their current perspectives on mental health, which typically rely solely on pathogens, to include salutogenesis -- a framework that includes the creation of health promotion and prevention. He stated that class and socio-economic status are aspects of social exclusion and are significant drivers of health equity.

Dr. Thompson recommended the Institute of Medicine's report entitled, "Prevention of Mental Disorders and Substance Abuse among Children, Youth, and Young Adults: Research Advances and Promising Interventions" because it provides a conceptual framework of mental health from a public health point of view. Practitioners must be mindful of elements that make a community healthy because today's children are born into complex circumstances, which include economic burdens, wars, and ecological disasters.

Dr. Thompson suggested that healthy communities practice ongoing dialogue with all of their members: generate leadership, actively shape their futures, embrace diversity, and know themselves and their history, connect people and resources, create a sense of belonging, and foster both creativity and innovation.

Dr. Maggi, an epidemiologist from Canada's Carleton University, discussed The Social Determinants of Preschoolers' Mental Health: Findings from the Canadian National Longitudinal Survey of Children and Youth. In the past decade, because of advances in assessment tools and the understanding of childhood development, there has been an increase in research concerning the mental health of pre-school aged children. Practitioners are now better equipped to detect problems earlier in life, and can become cognizant of mental health predictors across the lifespan. Mental health issues that emerge later in life typically are an accumulation of an individual's predisposing biology, interpersonal experiences, and social context. Recently, too, there has been increased appreciation in understanding social-emotional functioning related to school success and later health outcomes in adulthood. Dr. Maggi advocates that research is needed to expose the social determinants that impact children's development.

Dr. Maggi reviewed highlights from the National Longitudinal Survey of Children and Youth (NLSCY) to explore the role of family and neighborhood characteristics in mental health outcomes among preschoolers. Using a nationally representative study based on Canada's demographics, the study's researchers examined how determinants at ages 2 and 4 predict anxiety/depression, aggression, and inattentive hyperactivity/impulsive behavior later, when children are 4 and 6 years old.

The results indicated that inattention hyperactivity/impulsivity, aggressive behaviors, and anxiety/depression among young children related to neighborhood satisfaction -- particularly how individuals think about their neighborhood as a place to rear children. If improving neighborhood satisfaction can improve children's mental health outcomes then efforts should be made to impact modifiable determinants. Research exploring intervention at the community level in Canada, such as early child education, has not yet been explored.

To improve the mental health of children, advocates should be attuned to modifiable social determinants of mental health -- especially the safety of neighborhoods. Dr. Maggi concluded by stating that researchers must continue to study the environments in which children are live because research neighborhood satisfaction plays an important role in their mental health.

Dr. Moore, a clinical psychologist and faculty member at the Adler School of Professional Psychology, presented a paper entitled Comparison of Mental Health Outcomes for Child Soldiers and Youth Gangs based on a Human Rights Perspective. She explained that, in American society, the public view of youth in gangs differs from that of children soldiers. This disparity alters the treatment that is recommended by professional literature for both groups.

Dr. Moore argues that the public view of these two groups should not be vastly different, since there are many commonalities between the groups. In both, children are selected because they are vulnerable due to macro-level social determinants like globalization, economic factors, and ecological breakdowns. These factors promote a conflictual environment that allows adult leaders to recruit children easily.

Literature suggests that youth gangs and child soldiers experience mental health issues, including post-traumatic stress disorder, depression, substance abuse, anger management, and poor social/emotional functioning. To mitigate these issues, investigators should look at the community in which they reside.

Presently, the preferred treatment of a child soldier incorporates disarming, de-mobilization, and re-integration. This process includes psychological treatment, community intervention, development of social skills, and job training. In contrast, the preferred mental health treatment for children in gangs consists largely of suppression via incarceration.

Dr. Moore asked, if there is a parallel between these populations, why then is there a difference in the mental health treatment approach for these clients? To answer this question, she turned the audience's attention to the literature and ethos.

Human rights literature stresses that child soldiers are child victims of adult activity, whereas youth gangs are typically viewed as adults regardless of their age. Therefore, Dr. Moore recommended the reconsideration of the mental health treatment of youth gangs in light of these parallels. She recommended that federal government develop new policies that would address the mental health needs of these children. Rehabilitation of youth gangs could improve the mental health of these children, their families, and the communities in which they live.

During the question and answer period, one participant suggested that there are undocumented workers like Latinos in the United States and Aboriginals in Canada, who are vulnerable to many of the same early childhood conditions described in the presentations. Another participant reiterated the importance of advocating for youth in both marginalized and mainstream communities.

SESSION 1.3 ABSTRACTS

Prevention of Mental Disorders and Substance Abuse Among Children, Youth, and Young Adults

Kenneth S. Thompson, MD

Center for Mental Health Services, Substance Abuse and Mental Health Services Administration, US Dept. of Health and Human Services, Washington, DC

The capacity to prevent behavioral health disorders and promote mental health across the life span has long been a dream of people concerned about the mental health of the nation.

It has been clear for a very long time that the provision of clinical services to individuals would never come close to meeting the needs of the population. There will never be enough practitioners, and practitioners will not ever be as effective as we would want them to be. A public health approach to mental health has been slow to develop, but has recently begun to establish itself.

This presentation will focus on recent developments in human ecological theory and praxis in the EU, US, and Canada that are increasing our capacity to identify and address the social processes (i.e., the "social determinants of mental health") that either promote or impinge on the development of our mental "capital."

Particular attention will be paid to work focused on children, adolescents, and young adults, including the recently released "Public Health Approach to Children's Mental Health" and the Institute of Medicine's report on the "Prevention of Mental Disorders and Substance Abuse Among Children, Youth, and Young Adults: Research Advances and Promising Interventions."

The Social Determinants of Preschoolers' Mental Health: Findings from the Canadian National Longitudinal Survey of Children and Youth

Stefania Maggi, PhD

Institute of Interdisciplinary Studies, Department of Psychology, Carleton University, Ottawa, Canada. Co-authors: D'Angiulli, A.; Babchishin, L.

A variety of mental health problems can be detected as early as the preschool years and these outcomes are predictive of mental health problems in adolescence and adulthood. While much attention has been directed towards the role of socialization within the family in determining mental health outcomes among young children, fewer studies have focused on the role of higher-level social determinants such as the broader community and the neighbourhood.

The present study explored the role that neighbourhood characteristics play in promoting mental health among preschoolers. In particular, we examined how neighbourhood safety and social cohesion predict anxiety/depression, aggression, and inattentive hyperactive/impulsive behaviours (IHIB) among a representative sample of 4-6 years old Canadian children.

We analyzed data from the Canadian National Longitudinal Survey of Children and Youth (NLSCY) where family socioeconomic status and neighbourhood characteristics were measured among 3,452 children between 2, 3, and 4 years of age from the first survey cycle that was completed in 1994/95. Mental health outcomes were assessed in the second survey cycle that was completed two years later in 1996/97, at which time children were 4, 5 and 6 years old respectively.

Analyses were performed using both sampling and bootstrap weights producing conservative predictive estimates. After controlling for important family and socio-economic characteristics, IHIB, aggression, and anxiety/depression were found to be related to maternal reports of neighbourhood satisfaction; males were more likely to be aggressive and display IHIB than females; and that older children tended to be less aggressive but more anxious/depressed than younger children.

Because it has been proven that the safety of neighbourhoods can be successfully improved, advocates should pay special attention to this modifiable social determinant of mental health.

Comparison of Mental Health Outcomes for Child Soldiers and Youth Gangs Based on Human Rights Perspectives

Nataka Moore, PsyD

Department of Training, Adler School of Professional Psychology, Chicago, IL.
Co-authors: Monique Link; Nancy Bothne.

This paper is aimed toward developing a research agenda that would prompt new policy impacting the mental health of children in the U.S. who are involved in gangs. It offers a theoretical foundation that relies on human rights principles to encourage the development of alternatives to costly punitive measures that will improve mental health outcomes among children vulnerable to gang influence.

According to Singer, author of the book Children at War, there are strong comparisons between child soldiers abroad and children involved in gangs in the United States. Despite so many overwhelming similarities between child soldiers and children in American gangs, children in American gangs are often penalized through their state or federal judicial system and are treated like criminals when internationally the preferred treatment for child soldiers is rehabilitation.

One of the guiding principles for offering child soldiers rehabilitation (i.e. mental health services) over the penal system is that according to the Optional Protocol to the CRC for Child Soldiers, their human rights were violated and thus according to human rights laws, they should receive reparations (i.e. rehabilitation).

Thus, when understanding mental health outcomes of child soldiers versus children in gangs, two research questions emerge: 1) Does punishment of child gang members result in poor mental health outcomes? 2) Does rehabilitation result in good mental health outcomes for child soldiers?

This presentation proposes that in response to these research questions the federal government may take an international human rights focus on children inducted into gangs as a guide to develop new policy that would more fully address the mental health needs of children in the form of mental health rehabilitation.

Concurrent Session 2: Awareness

2.1: SOCIAL DETERMINANTS OF REFUGEES' EXPERIENCE
Presenters: Thuy Pham, PsyD; Marianne Joyce, MA

SUMMARY

The Social Determinants of Refugees' Experience session led by Dr. Thuy Pham and Ms. Marianne Joyce highlighted the formidable mental health challenges and outcomes faced by refugees and asylees in the United States. Their presentations served to counter negative stereotypes about these individuals, by explaining the systems, policies, and funding limitations that make integration difficult and lengthy.

Refugees are children, adolescents, adults, and families who involuntarily leave their native country due to persecution, violence, human rights abuses, and/or disasters. After arrival in a country of asylum, the United Nations High Commissioner for Refugees (UNHCR) directs emigration and ensures that registered refugees will not be forcibly returned to their country of origin.

Of the three available options (voluntary repatriation, local integration into country of asylum, and resettlement), resettlement is the most useful yet least utilized. This stressful process could take weeks, months, or years to complete due to paperwork, testing, medical tests, and numerous interviews that determine eligibility and may compound previous trauma and anxiety.

Barriers to resettling in Illinois are numerous. It is expected that refugees will become self-sufficient within a year, but they are generally provided with insufficient monetary support.

Community agencies must absorb shortfalls between available federal funds and refugee needs, while simultaneously struggling with financial issues themselves. In addition, affordable and safe housing may be far from the city and this, too, creates employment and transportation barriers. Often, refugees from different countries are encouraged to live together so they may enjoy housing closer to the city and reduce stressful home environments.

Although funding has recently been increased, the amount and duration of money received by these individuals in the 1970's was far greater than that which is available today. Thus, refugees experience additional stress and further tax emotional resources. Furthermore, many refugees are unfamiliar with the concept of therapy and may under use mental health services that are available.

These issues constitute significant barriers to employment and self-sufficiency when a psychiatric issue interferes with functioning. Similarly, there is a lack of funding for English as a Second Language (ESL) services. Language instruction may, therefore, be offered only during limited periods and be accompanied by long waiting lists. Dr. Pham made several recommendations to address these structural barriers – e.g., increasing funding for medical assistance, case management, bilingual therapists, and ESL services. She further observed that funding for social services should include non-competitive grants and training for mental health providers.

Ms. Joyce's presentation focused on asylees who face similar challenges when involuntarily immigrating to the United States. Many are torture survivors and have long-lasting physical, emotional, and cognitive deficits flowing from their experiences. Further, they are vulnerable because their social support networks have been disrupted. In order to adapt, survivors use avoidance and isolation coping strategies, while developing hyper-vigilance and mistrust of others as a means of self-protection.

However, environmental factors can ameliorate the psychological effects of torture. For example, obtaining political asylum represents safety and hope, while restoring a sense of control. Asylum status also includes the right to petition to reunite with family, eligibility for financial aid, and ability to obtain citizenship rather than returning to the native country where torture could reoccur.

Obtaining political asylum, however, is an arduous process and may re-traumatize survivors. Asylees bear the burden of proving past persecution or well-founded fears of persecution at times when many are not psychologically prepared to relive the trauma. Further, several policy changes have made this process adversarial. The 1996 Illegal Immigration Reform Act expedites the removal and detention of non-citizens with false or inadequate papers. Detention of asylum seekers is common

(32%) and results in diminished chances of success. While being detained, medical neglect may lead to death. If granted a trial, asylum decisions vary dramatically across judges, federal courts of appeal, Bureau of Immigration appeals or even within the same administrative office. Recommendations for facilitating the process of asylum-seeking included greater activism through partnerships with survivors to increase the availability of legal representation and political reform - particularly modification of the Refugee Protection Act of 2010.

Both speakers believe that community integration is an important factor in promoting mental health within the refugee population of Chicago. Connecting with others from similar cultural backgrounds often leads to better outcomes. Empowering communities to develop grassroots networks to foster relationships with incoming refugees is necessary. Similarly, national conferences and research with policy makers, funders, and mental health professionals will help develop better interventions. Concurrently, training and teaching judges and attorneys about refugee issues is of paramount importance. Ultimately, the goal of these changes is to meet the standard of the Universal Declaration of Human Rights by providing everyone with a proper standard of living, well-being, and security.

SESSION 2.1 ABSTRACTS

The Refugee Resettlement Process: Impact of Policy and Funding on the Mental Health of Chicago's Refugees

Thuy Pham, PsyD

Department of Training, Adler School of Professional Psychology, Chicago, IL

The United States Refugee Resettlement Process begins when refugees flee their country of origin due to fear of persecution, war, conflict, ethnic cleansing, and/or targeted persecution. Their journey is fraught with stress and trauma as they are forced to leave families, friends, and their country of origin behind.

Refugees typically wait in a host country to determine whether they will be integrated into the host country, returned back to their country of origin, or resettled in a third country. While being resettled into the United States is often the best and only option for refugees, many do not realize the hardships they will face until they arrive in our country and are expected to obtain employment within eight months to a year.

This is a challenging task given the current recession. In the 1970's federal funding in the form of cash and medical assistance for refugees used to cover a thirty-six month period. Since then federal funding for refugees had not increased despite our government continuing to accept thousands of refugees per year.

The federal government has transferred much of the responsibility to the states and local resettlement agencies to come up with the funds to support refugees. Although there has been an increase in federal cash and medical assistance this fiscal year, it does not cover the continued needs of refugees in Chicago.

With Illinois' economic problems and significant budget cuts, the state cannot financially support refugees entirely. Refugees are at risk for cumulative trauma without adequate and continued federal support. Many refugees face barriers to self-sufficiency including lack of childcare options, lack of employment opportunities, and inability to speak English-which further contributes to refugee stress.

Federal funding for local resettlement agencies and communities is critical for promoting and sustaining refugees' overall health-especially their mental health.

Social Determinants Affecting Torture Survivors Seeking Political Asylum in the U.S.

Marianne Joyce, MA

Heartland Alliance Marjorie Kovler Center, Chicago, IL. Co-author: Mary Fabri, PsyD

The terrorist attack on 9-11 has had many profound consequences across the United States. This presentation will provide an analysis of the macro-, meso-, and micro- consequences of this event on torture survivors seeking political asylum in the U.S.

The forces operating at the macro level include a culture of fear which contributed to changes in immigration policy, including: increases in detention of asylum seekers; new policies on state security that are in contradiction with international law, such as extraordinary rendition; the Guantanamo military detention center and justification for the use of torture.

Meso-systems have enormous influence in the quality of life of torture survivors. The Department of Homeland Security (DHS) determines whether an applicant remains in the U.S. or will be deported. Legal representation increases a survivor's chances of having a successful asylum claim, but many have no access to attorneys. DHS often deems asylum seekers ineligible for work permits resulting in a one to five year legal process in conditions of chronic poverty, dependence and vulnerability. If they are able to obtain employment, it is usually below their educational and work experience and results in additional loss of status and self-worth.

At the micro- level, the individual survivor endures the emotional, physical, cognitive and spiritual effects of torture. Fear, mistrust, grief and isolation often interact with meso-system structures such as families, employment, schools, health care providers and other service groups. While torture treatment centers work to promote stability and capacity for integration, meso- and macro-systems often contribute to increased vulnerability and persistent fear and are counter-productive to assistance efforts.

In conclusion, this presentation will propose a model of collaboration and multidisciplinary strategies to effectively engage, not only the survivor, but the systems that directly impact their resilience and hope about the future.

2.2: SOCIAL DETERMINANTS OF DEPRESSION

Presenters: Emily Mendenhall, MPH, MA; Krysia Mossakowski, PhD

SUMMARY

During the awareness-themed session entitled the Social Determinants of Depression, Ms. Emily Mendenhall, and Dr. Krysia Mossakowski presented on their respective research.

Ms. Mendenhall discussed The Social Determinants of Distress: Understanding the Impact of Interpersonal Violence on Depression among Mexican-American Diabetics. She reported that diabetics are two times more likely to be depressed than non-diabetics are. Ms. Mendenhall acknowledged that, while the rates of depression across ethnic groups are similar, the extent to which African American and Latino diabetics seek treatment for depression is significantly lower than Caucasians.

With respect to diabetes, she stated that studies on Mexican and Mexican-American diabetics demonstrate that individuals use powerful emotions to explain diabetes causality. Her preliminary ethnographic study revealed the following. Mexican-Americans implicate stress and distress as causal to diabetes by linking diabetes with emotions [susto (fright), coraje (anger), sadness, depression, and stress]. Those who report coraje in personal explanatory models are more likely to be depressed. Women are more likely than men to link coraje with diabetes causality in these models. Additionally, more women display symptoms of depression than men do.

From this preliminary study, the researcher and her collaborators also found that more than half of the women reported some form of physical, verbal, or emotional abuse; many of these women linked abuse with coraje; and, women who reported abuse as causal to diabetes also displayed symptoms of depression. From this, the presenter hypothesized that women use emotions to communicate abuse and that specific reporting of coraje may function as a marker of abuse or risk for depression.

The second presenter of the session, Dr. Mossakowski, spoke about Exploring the Long-term Relationship between Disadvantaged Family Background and Symptoms of Depression. She stated that, past research implicates disadvantaged parental socioeconomic status earlier in life as a risk factor for symptoms of depression in young adulthood and adulthood. Social stress theory maintains that living in an economically disadvantaged family environment increases one's vulnerability to stress. Dr. Mossakowski indicated that this vulnerability might then lead to psychological distress and symptoms of depression. She then incorporated the additional construct of self-esteem into her discussion, citing research suggesting that stronger self-esteem significantly decreases the likelihood of developing symptoms of depression.

Given that people from disadvantaged backgrounds unfavorably compare themselves to individuals from higher socioeconomic backgrounds, there is the potential for weakening self-esteem in lower socioeconomic individuals. Dr. Mossakowski went on to report that the influence of family socioeconomic status is stronger after childhood because of social class awareness in adolescents and young adults. Then, she examined whether levels of self-esteem during the transition to adulthood explains why parental education and parental occupational prestige have far-reaching effects on levels of depressive symptoms in young adults and inquired whether the relationship between disadvantaged parental status earlier in life and subsequent symptoms of depression may be explained by the stress of long-standing poverty.

Overall, her results suggested that self-esteem is a substantial mediating mechanism with respect to the relationship between earlier parental education and depressive symptoms. Dr. Mossakowski also observed the importance of acknowledging the length of time that a family has experienced poverty to understand the chronic stress of economic hardship.

SESSION 2.2 ABSTRACTS

The Social Determinants of Distress: Understanding the Impact of Interpersonal Violence on Depression Among Mexican Diabetics

Emily Mendenhall, MPH, MA, PhD (candidate)

Department of Anthropology, Northwestern University, Evanston, IL. Co-authors: Alicia Fernandez, MD; Elizabeth Jacobs, MD MPP

Depression is prevalent among patients with diabetes and increases the morbidity and mortality associated with this chronic illness. Our previous ethnographic research in Chicago suggests that psychosocial stress related to interpersonal violence contributes to clinical depression and poorer diabetic outcomes. To further explore this relationship we conducted a cross-sectional survey of 404 first and second generation Mexican American patients with diabetes seeking care at safety-net clinics in Chicago and San Francisco.

We asked patients about what they thought causes diabetes, including biomedical factors, such as diet and obesity, and non-biomedical factors, such as strong emotions and experience with interpersonal violence. The survey also assessed symptoms of depression using the PHQ-9 and a measure of glycemic control (hemoglobin A1c) was abstracted from electronic medical records.

We found that 301 (75%) people reported strong emotions as a cause of diabetes; 114 (28%) people identified abuse as a cause of diabetes; and 112 (28%) people reported both emotion and abuse as a contributor to diabetes. We conducted multivariate logistic regression to examine the relationship between beliefs about emotion and interpersonal violence, depression, and hemoglobin A1c controlling for demographic factors.

We found that patients who held non-traditional beliefs were more likely to have better glycemic control and fewer depressive symptoms than those who did not hold these beliefs. Nonetheless, the relationship between such beliefs and reduced depression symptomology became more evident when belief in abuse causing diabetes was put into the model. This suggests that the belief that abuse causes diabetes is an indicator of increased risk of depression. This cross-disciplinary work highlights the mechanisms by which social determinants contribute to depression in the chronically ill. Our study is relevant for the conference on the social determinants of mental health, as it bridges disciplinary, professional, and sectoral perspectives and illustrates the potential pathways by which social context impacts mental health and well-being.

Exploring the Long-Term Relationship Between Disadvantaged Family Background and Symptoms of Depression

Krysia Mossakowski, PhD

Department of Sociology, University of Miami, Coral Gables, FL

An area of the literature on the social determinants of mental health has documented that disadvantaged socioeconomic status is associated with symptoms of depression.

Depression is one of the most disabling mental disorders because the symptoms can drastically impair social functioning throughout people's lives, and the onset of depression usually occurs during young adulthood. More longitudinal research is necessary to focus on stressors and psychological resources during the transition to adulthood to advance our understanding of why there is a long-term relationship between earlier family social conditions and a young adult's mental health.

From the standpoint of social stress theory, being raised in an economically disadvantaged family environment not only increases exposure to chronic stressors, but also vulnerability to stress because of limited psychosocial resources, which in turn, lead to symptoms of depression.

Using social stress theory and data from the U.S. National Longitudinal Survey of Youth, this study focuses on mediating mechanisms from the transition to adulthood that help to explain why disadvantaged family background predicts higher levels of subsequent depressive symptoms at ages 29 to 37.

Results indicate that parental education and parental occupational prestige have significant inverse relationships with depressive symptoms, over and above demographic factors and prior depressive symptoms. Furthermore, low self-esteem at ages 15 to 23 largely explains the relationship between low parental education and depressive symptoms. The depressive effect of low parental occupational prestige is substantially explained by the duration of poverty status. Poverty duration across 16 years is assessed in this study – a longer span of time than other studies in the mental health literature. Overall, the implications of these findings are that policymakers and social welfare interventions should target self-esteem enhancement and the prevention of poverty spells during the journey to adulthood.

2.3: RACIAL/ETHNIC/GENDER-BASED BIAS AS SOCIAL DETERMINANTS OF MENTAL HEALTH

Presenters: Scott Anderson, MHSc; Christy A. Rentmeester, PhD; Mayumi Nakamura, PsyD

SUMMARY

The Racial/Ethnic/Gender-Based Bias as Social Determinants session heightened awareness of mental health considerations, when working with multicultural individuals -- particularly those who identify as being bisexual, an individual of color, or Asian American.

The session commenced with Scott Anderson, a researcher from the Centre for Addiction and Mental Health in Canada, who discussed the Social Determinants of Mental Health for Bisexual People. The presentation highlighted that bisexual mental health outcomes are poorer than those of gay or lesbian people, especially in areas like anxiety, depression, self-harm, suicidality, and self-rated access to mental health services. The research team utilized a community-based participatory action research project to identify intrapersonal, interpersonal, and social determinants of bisexual mental health.

At the macro-level, the study noted that social structures such as bi-phobia and mono-sexism paradigms exist, and that common societal attitudes and beliefs stigmatize bisexuality. On an interpersonal level, family, friends, and co-workers may have limited knowledge of bisexual individuals. Additionally, at the intrapersonal level, bisexual individuals themselves may struggle with their own identity, self-acceptance, and self-empowerment.

The community-based participatory action research project suggested that bisexual people in Ontario, Canada, have unique mental health determinants especially those related to the lack of social acknowledgment and support of bisexuality. Furthermore, social attitudes about bisexuality may lead to barriers to accessing mental health services. Structural changes are needed to improve social attitudes towards bisexuality and in turn to improve bisexual mental health services in Ontario.

Consistent with the conference theme "Awareness to Action," the presenter proposed some interventions, namely: anti-discrimination public education campaigns, sexual health education in the community, training for service providers, and establishment of support groups.

Dr. Christy A. Rentmeester, a philosopher and bioethicist from Creighton University, continued the session by discussing Legacies of Oppression and Mental Health among People of Color. She encouraged students to understand the intersection of clinical practice and health justice. She emphasized that racial/ethnic inequalities often intersect with the underserved mentally ill populations.

In particular, those individuals with chronic mental illness are typically underserved. She believes that this domain of mental health goes unpublicized and unrecognized by the community. In her opinion, communities face a series of micro-aggression that traumatize repeatedly. Traumatic stress, like legacies of racism and oppression, can obliterate one's temporal sense of self and one's ancestral connection. When these messages are passed on in the community, individuals may feel isolated, alienated, or disconnected.

Dr. Rentmeester suggested that inequalities have been addressed in the cultural competency literature found in the field of bioethics. Racial and ethnic inequality in health care can be ameliorated overtime by educating clinicians in the classroom, providing background cultural information within the clinical curriculum, and encouraging racial/ethnic minorities to become healthcare professionals. However, this approach is limited because it does not take into account how legacies of colonialism have damaged some communities.

Inspired by post-colonial thought, Dr. Rentmeester maintained that bioethics is able to augment cultural competency training. First, medicine and science possess the knowledge and tools to identify and measure physical features of people. Second, medicine and science use their authority to render judgment of what is considered normal and what deviates from normal. Third, medicine and science -- through knowledge and practice -- sought to establish and perpetuate the presumed inferiority of colonized people. Subsequently, awareness of these circumstances helped health care professionals to better understand the roots of health care inequalities.

Dr. Mayumi Nakamura, a clinical psychologist and faculty member at the Adler School of Professional Psychology, concluded the session by discussing Suicide of Asian Americans: Pressure to Succeed. She noted that information on this topic is limited, and traditionally individuals have stereotypes of Asian Americans, which limit their ability to conduct objective research.

She explained that the demographics of Asian Americans are very diverse. In 2006, suicide was the ninth leading cause of death for Asian Americans in the United States. High suicide rates are associated with Asian Americans who are under pressure to perform, conform, and succeed. Specifically, there is a high level of parental pressure and expectation to succeed academically to secure a valuable career. In particular, students from immigrant families feel pressured because of the sacrifices made for them by their family members. Pressure not only comes from parents and other family members, but also from society at large.

Asian Americans are reluctant to access assistance from mental health providers. To appreciate the lower utilization rates, Dr. Nakamura identified cultural factors that act as barriers to mental health treatment access.

Specifically, she discussed the stigma related to mental illness -- e.g., emotional illness viewed as shameful, a strong desire to preserve face, and a concern that mental illness diagnosis would negatively affect one's social network.

When later asked by an audience member for specific intervention recommendations, Dr. Nakamura advocated for multi-disciplinary team collaboration, especially one involving primary care physicians. She stated this is necessary because Asian Americans typically present to their primary care physicians with somatic complaints and, therefore, would need to be referred for assessment by a mental health professional.

SESSION 2.3 ABSTRACTS

The Social Determinants of Mental Health for Bisexual People

Scott Anderson, MHSc

Social Equity and Health Research Section Centre for Addiction and Mental Health, Toronto, Canada.

Research indicates that bisexual people report higher rates of anxiety, depression, poor mental health, suicidality, alcohol misuse, and self-harming behaviour and lower on measures of quality of life, emotional well-being, and social support than heterosexual people, and in many cases, than gay men and lesbians as well.

To date, little research has addressed what the causes of these differences in mental health and emotional well-being may be.

Drawing on the results from a community based participatory research project which included focus groups and semi-structured interviews with 55 bisexual people across Ontario, Canada, this presentation will discuss what bisexual people identify as key social determinants of mental health.

This presentation will examine the intersections of macro, meso, micro-level social determinants of mental health participant's identified, as well as both the positive and negative determinants of mental health.

These determinants include discrimination (monosexism and biphobia), social support, isolation, identity disclosure/nondisclosure, invisibility, internalized homophobia and biphobia, relationships with partners, and media representations of bisexuality on participants' mental health.

Potential interventions addressing the macro, meso and micro level social determinants of mental health for bisexual people will be presented.

Legacies of Oppression and Mental Health Among People of Color

Christy A. Rentmeester, PhD

Center for Health Policy and Ethics, Creighton University School of Medicine, Omaha, NE

Racial and ethnic inequalities result in people with mental illness being denied access to and being underserved in the health care system.

The intersections of these two kinds of inequalities have not received much attention beyond statistics; this article canvasses some of the background, recent trends, and current responses to these inequalities.

One place racial and ethnic inequalities have been examined by bioethicists is in the cultural "competency" literature. Underservice to people with mental illnesses has also been a focus of scholarly and public advocacy, particularly in campaigns to destigmatize mental illness.

I offer key concepts, inspired by postcolonial thought, to aid fuller consideration of the concept stigma among patients of color with mental illnesses in marginalized communities and suggest reasons for why health professions education should critically reconsider lessons in cultural "competency" and focus more on population-based goals of moral repair to promote therapeutic relationships between clinicians and patients and to promote health justice in underserved communities.

Suicide of Asian Americans: Pressure to Succeed

Mayumi Nakamura, PsyD

Department of Training, Adler School of Professional Psychology, Chicago, IL.
Co-author: Euhna Kim, PhD

This presentation begins with an acknowledgement of the diversity within the Asian American population as well as the limited information available on suicide among this particular group.

The term Asian American group refers to a diverse group of people, with varying cultures, languages, histories, views of mental health illness, and views of suicide (Leong, Leach, Yeh, & Chou, 2007).

There has been an increase of studies examining suicide of Asian Americans, but still information regarding this topic is very limited.

Recent data on the high suicide rates among Asian American are resulting in an increase in public attention to this important issue (Noh, 2003). According to Centers for Disease Control and Prevention (CDC, 2009), suicide was the 8th leading cause of death for Asian Americans compared to the 10th for White Americans in 2006.

Furthermore, suicide is the second leading cause of death among Asian American women (aged 15-24). It is also important to note that Asian Americans, like other people of color, underutilize mental health services so the level of their stress tends to be more severe when they are first seen by clinicians (Chen, Sullivan, Lu & Shibusawa, 2003; Kearney, Draper & Baron, 2005), with suicide being a particular concern (Liu, Yu, Chang, & Fernandez, 1990).

Moreover, ethnic minority clients including Asian American are less likely to disclose their suicide ideation than European Americans (Morrison & Downey, 2000).

Concurrent Session 3: Awareness

3.1: CULTURE AS A SOCIAL DETERMINANT
Presenters: Neely Myers, PhD; Ronald Markwardt, PhD

SUMMARY

In the Culture as a Social Determinant session, Drs. Myers and Markwardt discussed how culture influences mental health with emphasis on comparing the impact of developing and industrialized nations on health outcomes. They also highlighted protective factors and interventions that ameliorate stress and increase stability.

The focus of Dr. Myers' presentation was cultural-based outcomes for individuals living with schizophrenia. Within the United States and other developed countries, this diagnosis is associated with poor outcomes and a nomadic lifestyle. For example, in Western countries, people with schizophrenia have high employment and often depend heavily on government assistance. Also, persons with schizophrenia face high institutionalization and substance use rates, experience violent crime, and confront social stigma.

On average, the lifespan of individuals with schizophrenia is 25 years shorter than their peers. Factors like these create a culture of chronicity and adoption of a sick role that maintains psychiatric symptoms. Although one-third of the individuals with schizophrenia remain chronically ill, and one-third attain complete remission, the remaining third achieve partial recovery.

In contrast, individuals living in developing countries are 1.5 times more likely to recover, with some countries having even better outcomes (e.g., India). Possible reasons include increased family involvement and advocacy, more accessible work roles, less pressure related to lowered economic expectations, encouragement to marry, and increased community cohesion and integration that exist in developing countries. By comparison, cultural factors associated with poor outcomes include migration, urban areas with limited affordable housing, high expressed emotion within the family, and stigma, which are factors more commonly seen in developed countries. As Dr. Neely stated, culture goes "beyond medicine" to influence outcomes.

According to the diathesis-stress model of schizophrenia, culture interacts with biology to produce symptoms. In this way, culture "gets under the skin" by influencing underlying physiological conditions. Specifically, the hypothalamic-pituitary-adrenal (HPA) axis involves the autonomic nervous system, stress hormones, and immune response. Individuals with schizophrenia have overactive stress responses and consequently have difficulty maintaining bodily homeostasis. Associated increases in cortisol and reduced ability to control stress response exacerbate symptoms.

Fortunately, there are a variety of complementary and alternative therapies available which are effective in promoting homeostasis by improving stress reduction. In addition, they decrease anxiety, depression, and cognitive issues while improving quality of life.

For example, yoga may reduce symptoms while increasing social and occupational functioning. Music therapy is another promising technique that improves anxiety, depression, and social functioning. Recent evidence suggests omega-3 fish oil supplements reduce psychosis conversion for 25% of adults. Mindfulness meditation also has the potential to reduce psychological distress and improve immune functioning. However, further research is needed to determine efficacy in schizophrenia.

Dr. Markwardt's presentation touched upon similar cultural themes in South East Asia. Specifically, his research examined the impact of Western culture on self-image and health in Thailand. To begin, Dr. Markwardt suggested that health and illness are not static; they are culturally determined constructs that exist on a continuum.

Similarly, stigma is defined as society's reaction to a disorder that varies with social mores. As such, the dynamic nature of culture results in ever-changing trends and social indicators over time. Further, culture, values, and mental health vary by generation and degree of industrialization as well. Unfortunately, the medical model may not be able to conceptualize health, while considering cultural factors.

In a similar vein, self-image is also impacted by culture and consists of four components: psychological (i.e., self-esteem), physical (i.e., body image), social (i.e., activities), and spiritual and emotional factors. The degree of Westernization has significantly affected the self-image of those living in South East Asia. For example, globalized values of beauty have shifted to include teeth/skin whitening and wearing cosmopolitan trendy clothing. These changes create stress between traditional culturally based values and new Western values. Despite these changes in self-image, Dr. Markwardt argues that cultural remnants or vestiges that give one a sense of rootedness and connectedness with the past remain within individuals.

In a recent pilot study, Dr. Markwardt asked participants in various Thai communities "What is mental health?" The responses included physical health, balanced mood, proper thinking, optimism, and morals. In Thai culture, social integration is synonymous with good mental health.

A related study demonstrated the impact of one's immediate surroundings on perceptions of mental health. For example, residents of a poor village may perceive poverty as unrelated to mental health, but those in a town with higher employment and economic status may perceive it as a determinant of mental health.

Both presenters described the influence of culture on perceptions and outcomes of mental health. It would be advantageous to incorporate these findings into future research studies on therapeutic interventions. Further, we must extend ourselves beyond the confines of traditional medical approaches to health and illness to properly tailor treatment to individuals of particular cultures.

SESSION 3.1 ABSTRACTS

Culture, Stress and Recovery from Schizophrenia: New Directions for Research

Neely Myers, PhD

School of Nursing, Center for the Study of Complementary and Alternative Therapies, University of Virginia, Charlottesville, VA

Schizophrenia is a pressing global mental health problem affecting 25 million people worldwide. Robust longitudinal research shows that social determinants of mental health -- or "cultural" factors like migration, urbanization, strength and scope of social support networks, community cohesion, and economic expectations and opportunities– influence schizophrenia outcomes. People in developing countries have more favorable outcomes than people in developed countries, leaving researchers to question why. Many existing theories indicate that certain cultural features like increased family involvement, greater availability of valued social roles, and reduced stigma may contribute to better outcomes. New research indicates neuropsychological mechanisms by which social distress may exacerbate symptoms of schizophrenia.

While the diathesis stress model has long been a part of the description of schizophrenia and we know that people with schizophrenia cannot handle even normal amounts of stress, advances in the field of psychoneuroimmunology provide a richer description of the ways that culture gets "under the skin" to impact the individual's experiences.

In the case of schizophrenia, oversensitivity to social stress and a dysregulation of the autonomic nervous system's balance, or homeostasis, creates a neural cascade of events that can trigger psychosis. This cascade of neural events leading from social stress to psychosis may be slowed or stopped using stress reduction techniques. Complementary therapies like yoga, mindfulness, nutritional support, and music therapy may help people with schizophrenia manage their stress and achieve better outcomes.

New assessment techniques offer researchers the tools needed to explore how complementary therapies impact stress, design interventions for the alleviation of schizophrenia symptoms, and assess the changes to the neurophysiological pathways involved.

Globalized Lifestyles: Examples of Ongoing Activity Changes, Physical Adaptations and Compensatory Mental Self-Images in South East Asia

Ronald Markwardt, PhD
Burapha University, Chonburi, Thailand

This paper draws on observations of the phenomenon of rapid industrialization of South East Asian countries. It describes the obvious effects of "Westernization" on lifestyle, and the varying levels of globalization in comparison to the Americas. Individual aspirations change with economic conditions. Availability of material goods, even food items and other lifestyle options are often accepted unwittingly by the youth and unwillingly by the elderly. In that context we review input from urban and rural communities regarding changing local definitions of mental health, patterns of support and individual awareness and response to services.

This paper then presents examples of how the cultural transitions toward "westernization" are affecting thinking patterns, including self-image and definitions of success (life goals). Rationalization of food choice and eating patterns are the primary examples used because the changes are also indicative of the trend toward chronic health problems such as obesity related diseases.

Anecdotes of college students in 5 Asian Countries with eating problems are used to illustrate the mechanisms and the pathways by which the social context impacts mental self-imagery and compensating behaviors. Examples of development or deterioration of self-image in response to social-class-specific stressors, such as the enforced dependency on debt based economy, minority group conflicts, and immigration pressures are presented as vignettes.

Finally, the paper will introduce the concept of maintaining "cultural remnants" as a possible anchoring device for healthy self-identity and mental stability. This is illustrated in policy and practice by some countries' conscious efforts to identify and promote traditional values as well as preserving patterns in behaviors, artifacts and architecture. Some hypotheses are made about how the formal education system can be adapted to encourage the development of the "socially integrated person" at different life stages.

3.2: INSTITUTIONAL BEHAVIORS & PUBLIC POLICY AS SOCIAL DE-TERMINANTS OF MENTAL HEALTH

Presenter: Sonya Jakubec, RN, BHScN, MN, PhD(c)

SUMMARY

During the awareness-themed session entitled Institutional Behaviors and Public Policy as a Social Determinant, PhD candidate Sonya Jakubec, delivered a presentation entitled Unraveling the Political and Social Organization of "the right to health and development."

Over the course her remarks, Ms. Jakubec discussed an intervention program in Ghana in which she is involved. Sponsored by a non-governmental organization, in this program Ms. Jakubec examined questions related to "the right to mental health and development." She astutely observed that the definition of health rights varies according to geographic location. To further illustrate this notion, Ms. Jakubec cited Paul Farmer who said, "the thing about human rights is that in the end you can't prove what should be considered a right."

For the remainder of her presentation, Ms. Jakubec spoke about her specific research interests. In considering the "right to health" and any rights indicators that may be woven into health policy, this study focuses on discovering work processes, discourses, and social practices that may produce subordination. Seeking to better understand various forms of governance, the study strives to locate sites for activism and change. Field observations, interviews, and document retrieval operation comprise the core of the data collection activities.

The study also revealed the significance of structural factors like social and local economic indicators. For these reasons, it is important to understand the ramifications of "the right o health and development: when one examines poverty and isolation within the context of various environments.

During the question and answer part of this session, one attendee asked how a researcher might avoid causing harm while conducting inquiries in another country. Ms. Jakubec responded by observing that focusing attention upon local cultural practices, rather than by inserting Western viewpoints into their work, could constitute a good starting point.

SESSION 3.2 ABSTRACT

Unraveling the Political and Social Organization of "The Right to Health and Development"

Sonya Jakubec, RN, BHScN, MN, PhD(c)

School of Nursing, Mount Royal University, Calgary, Canada.

Global justice and human rights language, of which there are a number of competing interests, is increasingly present in mental health promotion work internationally. Attending to human rights concerns is important for those advocating for mental health (and other health issues) at grassroots and international levels (Farmer, 2003). Funding and accountability in mental health and development depends upon workers' knowledgeable communication of these notions and deliverables in the name of "the right to health".

What happens at the intersection of the discourse and mental health/development practice indeed legitimizes some notions of rights, and obscures others. In this paper I introduce the problematic "right to health" discourse in mental health and development, at one site of work in the field, in order to unravel this complex weave of political and social organization. What I explicate through an institutional ethnography (Smith, 1987, 1999, 2002), is how diverse "human rights" expressions arise in academic, political and the international development sectors and how these expressions of "rights" are experienced in the field of mental health work.

My point of entry for this exploration is the work of a non-governmental development organization that advocates internationally for mental health and development. Through this site I examine the discourses in action, on the ground, and trace the connections between local health work and the global "right to mental health" discourse. Exploration of how the interests and discourses are brought to bear on every day practices in the field yields important findings about how the "right to mental health" is brought into action through economic indicators of health, and how alternative discourses are necessarily obscured in the process.

This paper provides an analysis of how existing health rights discourse and practices are enabling, helpful, limiting and, at times, harmful to actual mental health and development. With these findings as a basis for discussion, I further unravel the more generalizable challenges for scholars of "the human right to health", and dilemmas for programmatic and social change for policy makers, funding program officers and health workers intent upon realizing the right to mental health for all.

3.3: MENTAL HEALTH CONSIDERATIONS IN LATINO COMMUNITIES
Presenters: Karen E. Peters, DrPH; Refugio Gonzales, MBA

SUMMARY

To heighten awareness of social determinants of mental health, Dr. Karen Peters and Mr. Refugio Gonzales discussed mental health considerations in rural and urban Latino communities in Illinois, United States.

Dr. Karen Peters, a public health researcher at the University of Illinois at Chicago, shared information regarding the Participatory Approaches to Community Mobilization around Mental Health and Chronic Diseases among Rural Hispanic Immigrants. Understanding rural Hispanic population in Illinois is worthy of attention because 84 of 102 Illinois counties are rural, and there is a known disparity among rural populations regarding health status and access to health services. Furthermore, the Hispanic population is the fastest growing underserved population both in Illinois and in the United States.

To date, researchers have a limited understanding of the health status of rural Hispanic immigrants -- particularly that of those who reside in the upper Midwest of the United States.

Dr. Peters suggested using a Community Based Participatory Action Research (CBPAR) iterative approach consisting of partnership formation, assessment, implementation, evaluation and dissemination. Consistent with the theme of the Social Determinants of Mental Health conference, this method increases awareness of issues influencing the community and identifies data to mobilize community action. Collaboration with community members also increases the chances of sustainability. It promotes the understanding that all knowledge resides in the community and researchers are only one entity in the co-learning process.

The goal of the CBPAR was to investigate the connections between mental and physical health and the role of acculturation among rural Hispanic/Latino immigrant populations in Illinois. The team conducted community assessments to help determine priorities and address needs. The team provided resources to implement community oriented projects. It enhanced an understanding and identified future needs through ongoing evaluation. CBPAR enabled the research team to assess the understanding of mental and physical health by rural immigrant Hispanics residing in Illinois. Results of participant surveys, small group discussions, and a community survey, identified that stress, depression, and anxiety were the main health concerns across levels of acculturation. These findings were disseminated to the local community by newsletter articles and through educational workshops.

Mr. Gonzales, the Director of Latino Affairs for Chicago Commission on Human Relations, discussed Latino Mental Health Literacy: Steps That Must Be Taken. Consistent with the goal of the conference, he advocated that professionals and community members should not work in isolation; instead, individuals should form inter-disciplinary teams to address the complexity of community needs. In turn, these partnerships could advocate for policy reform.

The Advisory Council on Latino Affairs (ACLA) is one of eight advisory councils under the Chicago Commission on Human Rights which are representative of a wider array of constituency groups across the City of Chicago. Each council serves as a liaison between the city government and community based social services, faith and civic based institutions. In particular, their duties include assisting the commission by designing education and enforcement programs for the implementation of policies to eliminate discrimination. The ACLA consists of several ad-hoc committees, including education, employment, health, housing, immigration, and youth.

Mr. Gonzales highlighted numerous barriers impeding one's ability to have Health Literacy, which was defined as the ability to gain access to understand and use information in ways that promote and maintain good health. These barriers may include lack of English proficiency, lack of bilingual/bicultural mental health providers, characteristics of treatment that are insensitive to culture, lack of awareness of treatment, lack of family support due to stigma, and socio-economic status limiting access to services.

The ACLA has implemented strategies to move from awareness to action in ameliorating this problem by using a social justice framework. First, the council conducted environmental scans of mental health providers who are able to provide services in Spanish. Second, the council is planning an annual Latino Mental Health Conference. Additionally, it is collaborating to establish and support a Latino Mental Health Professional Network in Chicago. As well, it is participating in educational forums with educational institutions to share information with the community.

Mr. Gonzales recommended that further research addressing mental health issues for undocumented and uninsured immigrants be undertaken. To become an agent of change, Mr. Gonzales stated professionals must recognize that, inevitably, mental health issues will affect everyone. Finally, it is important to identify the institutions within our community that are able to provide comprehensive mental health services.

During the question and answer period, one participant suggested that Latino communities and other minorities face similar barriers in the United States. Other participants advocated for the collaboration of academic, institutional, governmental, and industrial partners to conduct research and stimulate change. Many audience members thanked the presenters for illuminating the complexities of working with both urban and rural Latino communities in Illinois.

SESSION 3.3 ABSTRACTS

Participatory Approaches to Community Mobilization Around Mental Health and Chronic Disease Among Rural Hispanic Immigrants

Karen E. Peters, DrPH

Division of Health Policy and Administration, School of Public Health Institute for Health, Research and Policy, University of Illinois at Chicago, Chicago, IL. Co-authors: Sergio Cristancho, PhD, Marcela Garces, MD, MSPH

In the US, the majority of existing research on psychological adjustment to chronic disease has been concentrated on the majority white population belonging to a relatively higher social status compared to African Americans or Hispanics. In addition, there are few studies that have targeted interventions to these vulnerable groups, in particular, among rural immigrant Hispanic populations.

This work reports on findings from two inter-related, multi-site studies aimed at community mobilization around mental health promotion and chronic disease prevention using a social determinants of health perspective. Both projects involved the formation of academic-community research partnerships, nine in total, to conduct a series of community-based participatory action research (CBPAR) projects to explore the relationships of acculturation and certain mental health conditions (e.g. stress, depression, health-related quality of life) with chronic diseases among a diverse group of rural Hispanic immigrant populations in Illinois.

Using the CBPAR approach, each community engaged in an assessment phase involving collection of data regarding the relationships between acculturation, mental health and chronic disease. In addition, five communities further developed small scale mobilization projects to address identified needs for health education/ health promotion strategies. All communities conducted evaluations of these efforts and created materials and products for dissemination that can be used in other similarly situated communities. Findings suggest that when academic-community based research is grounded in a social justice framework, Hispanic community members, in collaboration with multiple community partners, can create and sustain programs. Specifically, programming must be family oriented, gender specific (when feasible), location neutral, linguistically and culturally relevant, and low to no cost.

The set of community research findings contribute to the need for additional studies that attend to the social determinants of health in program development particularly for Hispanic immigrants who experience difficulties in their mental and physical health due to the assimilation process.

Latino Mental Health Literacy: Steps That Must Be Taken

Refugio Gonzales, MBA

Director/Community Liaison, Advisory Council on Latino Affairs, City of Chicago Commission on Human Relations, Chicago, IL. Co-authors: Rudy Espinoza; Mario Garcia; Ana Gil-Garcia

Among the duties of the Advisory Council on Latino Affairs of the City of Chicago (ACLA) is "to act as a liaison between city government and community to promote cooperation between the two". The Latino Council has taken steps forward to reinforcing collaboration between city and the extended Latino community that compresses more than 45% of the city of Chicago.

After working with psychology interns coming from a local educational institution, the ACLA decided to create the Health Committee to deal with issues affecting the Latino communities, especially mental health illiteracy.

Understanding that health literacy is a relevant precondition that supports day-to-day people's decisions on health-related issues, the Latino community is still very vulnerable to any decisions they make in regard to their own physical conditions and wellbeing due to the lack of health literacy and communication. Many factors impact Latinos on health literacy: immigration issues (i.e. deportation), cultural competency, language barriers, family myths and prejudices, traditions, education, among others.

The ACLA health committee's first task was to research on Latino depression. The crude reality confirmed what is known. Latinos do not speak about depression; do not know what health agencies to go to, what resources to consult, and what health implications develop from any type of mental condition.

Based on those findings, the committee has focused on delineating mental health literacy strategies within the context of intercultural and interpersonal communication to address vulnerability of Chicago Latinos. Additional strategies are co-sponsoring the Latino Mental Health Conference, participating and supporting Latino Mental Health Professional Network, continuing the relationship with existing education institutions, creating an educational forum to educate the general public on the issues of mental health, and lastly training Latino communities on cultural and linguistic competence about health concerns without cultural differences obstructing the conversation.

Concurrent Session 4: Action

4.1: THEORY TO PRACTICE
Presenters: Matthew Smith, PhD; Rahul Mediratta, MSc; Rochelle Burgess MPhil/PhD Candidate

SUMMARY

During the action-themed session entitled Theory to Practice, Dr. Matthew Smith, Mr. Rahul Mediratta, and PhD candidate Rochelle Burgess presented their respective work. Dr. Smith examined When Theory Meets Practice: Historical Perspectives on Social Approaches to Mental Illness. He reported that the British people consider mental illness more damaging than heart disease and noted that its annual costs are approximately £12 billion or 1% of the national economy. Given this reality, Dr. Smith acknowledged that mental health is an issue that is of enormous concern to health policy makers, physicians, and the public.

He argued that numerous political, economic, and scientific factors undermine preventive mental health policies, and that people disagree about which specific factors cause mental illness and about how to address those factors. He outlined a history of mental illness preventative efforts, dating back to the mid 1700's and noted the long history of such strategies in the United States.

Dr. Smith stated that today's attempts to prevent mental health problems must deal with difficult questions like how to define mental illness, which social determinants are most pathological, and how to take political action to address mental illness. He also discussed the geographical distribution of mental illness, which he stated could reveal information pertaining to the cause of mental illness.

Dr. Smith concluded his talk by emphasizing the importance of history within the context of mental health and by encouraging dialogue as a vehicle through which future action may arise.

Mr. Mediratta's talk focused on Strategic Policy and Population Health: Interministerial and intersectoral collaboration to improve the social determinants of mental health and addictions in Ontario. The objective of his research is to support governments and others in developing population health strategies.

Mr. Mediratta and his collaborators hope to generate valuable knowledge and theory about government strategies for improving population health and health equity; strategies for interministerial and intersectoral collaboration to improve the social determinants of health; and strategies related to mental health and addictions in Ontario.

The speaker noted that the social determinants of health and mental health affect individuals and groups. Early childhood development, education, income, employment, working conditions, stress, social support, social inclusion and exclusion, gender, culture, food security are involved. Mr. Mediratta presented a diagram by Dahlgren & Whitehead (1991) to demonstrate the notion that approximately 75% of the factors responsible for health occur outside the health care system. He noted that disadvantaged groups experience disproportionate rates of mental illness and addiction.

He then went on to discuss Health Alliance Plans (HAP). Specifically, he proposes two contemporary approaches to HAP strategy. These include targeting public policies by embedding Health Impact Assessment (HIA) in policies outside the health sector and targeting a health problem by 'joining up' government ministries to coordinate policies or create new policies outside of the health sector.

The final presenter for this session was Ms. Burgess, whose talk was entitled Can a Social Determinants approach to mental health be actualized? Exploring precursors to a long needed transition.

The focus of this presentation was upon the barriers confronted during implementation of a social determinants of health approach to policy. She examined a mental health program in South Africa. She noted that developing countries provide many case studies about endemic issues like violence, poverty, and gender inequality. In South Africa, especially, extreme poverty, violence, and HIV/AIDS impede progress in addressing mental health issues.

Ms. Burgess presented a case study of a rural outreach program that brings services (e.g., training workshops that provide coping mechanisms to support mental health in relation to HIV or AIDS, anxiety disorders, and suicide) to the hardest to reach communities in South Africa. She also spoke about moving the treatment from an emphasis on merely coping to an emphasis on transformation.

Finally, this speaker addressed hindrances to the social determinants approach to mental health. These include the notion that the discourse surrounding mental health is highly medicalized; and the continued resistance to a social determinants approach to general health and well-being.

SESSION 4.1 ABSTRACTS

When Theory Meets Practice:
Historical Perspectives on Social Approaches to Mental Illness

Matthew Smith, PhD

Centre for Medical History, University of Exeter, Exeter, United Kingdom. Co-author: Edmund Ramsden, PhD

In December 2009, the British government announced a major shift in mental health policy. Describing depression as more harmful to the nation's health than heart disease, it stated that one of the cornerstones of the ten-year strategy was to find ways to prevent depression.

Identifying and eliminating the social determinants of depression were highlighted as key aspects of the program. The desire to tackle the social determinants of mental illness is not a recent phenomenon. In February 1963, President Kennedy also described how the greatest threat to the American health was no longer infectious diseases, but mental illness. Kennedy, and many prominent American psychiatrists, believed that understanding the social causes of mental illness was fundamental to this struggle, and argued that psychiatry would have to engage with sociologists, psychologists, politicians, educators, and others in order to prevent its spread.

The term used to describe this multi-disciplinary, socially-focused approach was social psychiatry. Although such thinking did inspire preventative legislation, by the early 1970s, the financial pressures of the Vietnam War and the energy crisis had many believing that prospects for social psychiatry were poor and, by the end of the decade, pharmaceutical approaches to mental illness dominated.

This paper describes the rise and fall of social psychiatry during the post-war period in the United States. It argues that many of the conditions that precipitated the emergence of social psychiatry then are present now. These include geopolitical turmoil, economic uncertainty, and distrust in biomedical approaches to mental illness. However, many of the factors that undermined the flowering of social psychiatry during this period also threaten social approaches to mental illness today. The history of social psychiatry during the 1960s can help prepare mental health professionals to deal with the challenges of addressing the social determinants of mental illness today.

Strategic Policy and Population Health: Interministerial and Intersectoral Collaboration to Improve the Social Determinants of Mental Health and Addictions in Ontario

Rahul Mediratta, MSc

Health Systems Strategy Division Mental Health and Addictions Unit, Ontario Ministry of Health and Long-Term Care, Ontario, Canada. Co-author: Lauren Bialystok, PhD

This research project intends to support governments and sectors with their population health strategies. The authors work in strategic policy development for Ontario's Ministry of Health and Long-Term Care. Their research is an assessment of strategies, barriers and further opportunities toward collaboration among 14 government ministries and their respective sectors to improve the social determinants of mental health and addictions (SDOMHA) in Ontario, Canada.

Governments increasingly prioritize population health and health equity. Poor outcomes in population health and health inequities are considered unjust and are costly.

To improve population health and health equity, governments and institutions emphasize improving the social determinants of health (SDOH). The SDOH, which are living conditions that impact the health of individuals and groups , indicate that population health status is affected only in part by health services and, thereby, ameliorable by broader social and public policy ministries and their sectors.

Governments are experimenting with different interministerial and intersectoral strategies, such as Health in All Policies (HiAP) strategies, to improve the SDOH. HiAP is a broad and horizontal policy-related strategy that aims to examine public policies that may harm or can protect and promote health.

Through a case study on Ontario's 10-Year Mental Health and Addictions Strategy, this study explores a possible approach to HiAP: target a health problem by 'joining up' ministries to coordinate or create new policies and 'joining up' sectors to coordinate action on the SDOH.

Can a Social Determinants Approach to Mental Health Be Actualized? Precursors to a Long Needed Transition

Rochelle Burgess MPhil/PhD Candidate

Institute of Social Psychology, Health, Community and Development Research Group, London School of Economics and Political Science, London, United Kingdom. Co-author: Catherine Campbell, PhD

As global attention turns to mental health, there is an increasing interest in the role of social determinants of mental illness. International movements to scale up mental health services in socially deprived settings have caused many to question the relevance of western-individualized approaches to non western settings where contributors to illness differ drastically (Summerfield & Vale, 2008).

It is likely that the inclusion of a more socially constructed approach to mental health would go a long way addressing the inconsistencies in current treatment approaches in these settings, and ensuring that the mental health needs of marginalized communities in developing country contexts are successfully met.

This paper begins with a brief discussion of how a social determinants approach to mental illness can better address the mental health needs of marginalized communities, though discussion of the challenges faced by a mental health programme in South Africa. It continues on to question the ability for a social determinants approach to mental illness to be recognized in the absence of a shift in the conceptualization of mental illness specifically, and health and illness more generally.

In particular, it points to two key areas where change must be achieved in order for a social determinants approach to be actualized: 1) Medicalized discourses surrounding mental health; 2) Uptake of the social determinants approach in health more broadly.

4.2: PREVENTION
Presenters: Lynda E. Frost, JD PhD; Linda Shak, MSW

SUMMARY

The Action: Prevention Session emphasized knowledge mobilization and the application of mental health research findings to real world settings. Lynda E. Frost, JD, PhD, Susan Stone, JD, MD, and Linda Shak, MSW, discussed evidence-based approaches in developing community interventions for managing psychological distress by identifying and modifying social contributors to negative health outcomes.

Specifically, Frost and Stone described behavioral health indicators guiding action in Austin/Travis County, Texas. The community created a task force to respond to several instances of white police officers shooting some African Americans who had psychiatric illness.

The task force concluded that a lack of community services contributed to the mismanagement of psychiatric treatment for the violence victims and others. To address this issue, a monitoring committee coordinated the community's planning and data development resources and promoted increased community awareness of existing conditions for a period of more than five years.

The task force employed several innovative tools to collect community data – including a system map that identified available mental health services, revealed the presence of overlapping programs, and confirmed the absence of needed services. Mapping further contributed to ascertaining potential trends capable of adversely affecting mental health – e.g., obesity in children residing in neighborhoods having a high concentration of fast-food restaurants and a dearth of grocery stores. Additionally, the task force used a "scorecard" to track relevant community goals and initiatives impacted by the data collected.

The task force identified appropriate indicators of community health using root cause analyses. Four specific indicators emerged – i.e.., percentage of inmates with mental illness, re-admission rates at public psychiatric hospitals, percentage of people with behavioral health needs and unstable housing, and percentage of emergency department re-admissions with diagnoses of substance use. An additional indicator – change in referrals for alternative services – will soon be added to the original list of four. The next step in the process will be to determine factors that may result in indicator fluctuations. To accomplish this task, individuals with mental illness will be interviewed. Collaborative funding from city, county, and national agencies will allow this project to be extended for an additional two years.

Similarly, Ms. Shak's work at the Prevention Institute looked at environmental structures that influenced mental health. For example, sexist billboards, availability of liquor stores, and a lack of play areas for children all have adverse implications for psychological health and may result in isolation, low self-esteem, substance abuse, and exclusion.

To be effective, interventions must address multiple ecological levels simultaneously at individual, organizational, and societal levels. Moreover, advocates must work in concert to encourage policy makers to change laws. Although recognizing community-based problems and finding solutions is of vital importance, Ms. Shak also emphasized a prevention continuum.

On the left is primary prevention, which means taking action before symptom onset. In this way, the likelihood of an incident, condition, or illness occurring is significantly reduced. Examples of successful primary prevention strategies are using seatbelts, smoking prevention, and efforts that result in reducing the levels of lead to which children are exposed.

In the middle of the continuum is secondary prevention, which involves a response after symptoms or the risk of illness or injury becomes present. Finally, on the right, there is a tertiary or "aftermath" segment, which is a response after illness or injury onset.

In San Mateo County, California, four overlapping prevention strategies were developed: enhance place (i.e., stable housing, safety); connect people (i.e., reduce exposure to violence); foster prosperity (i.e., reduce stigma); and expand partnerships (i.e., engage government sector). Such strategies need to overlap because community problems are often multi-faceted. For example, community parks cannot be used if residents fear widespread violence.

Following this strategy, the community of Upper Falls, New York, developed a solution for the loss of a grocery store due to fire. As a result of the catastrophe, low median income residents confronted indefinite lack of access to affordable and healthy groceries. However, partnerships with the mayor, Tops, and Partners Through Food led to construction of a new grocery store that replaced the original one and resulted in an increased consumption of fruits and vegetables within the community. Review of this example and similar past successful interventions, generates a spectrum of prevention that includes influencing policy, changing organizational practices, fostering coalitions and networks, educating providers, solving multiple problems, and strengthening individual knowledge and skills.

In keeping with the mission of the conference regarding turning awareness into action, these speakers provided specific suggestions for engaging in successful community-based intervention work. They showed the many benefits of using an integrative, team-based, and holistic approach to provide well-integrated community solutions to difficult problems.

The work of Drs. Frost and Stone demonstrated the advantages of well-tailored intervention directed toward specific populations. Collaborating with community representatives for buy-in, trust building, and data collection is essential. Part of this process involves disseminating information to the community to increase transparency, facilitate communication, and obtain feedback. For example, the results of the "scorecard" can be placed on a website for interested parties to read. Doing that demonstrates the usefulness of a specific intervention and engages others in the process. In this way, interventions to address social and structural barriers to mental health can be properly implemented and become sustainable.

SESSION 4.2 ABSTRACTS

Using Community Behavioral Health Indicators to Guide Action on the Social Determinants of Mental Health

Lynda E. Frost, JD, PhD

Hogg Foundation for Mental Health, University of Texas at Austin, Austin, TX. Co-author: Susan Stone, J.D., M.D.

Research often focuses on the link between social determinants and health status, such as lack of stable housing and poor mental health. It is important to take the next step and move beyond a focus on individuals to delineate the political and social context of health and health disparities.

Public policy affects social determinants and can be a powerful tool in eliminating disparities and improving health. In order to gauge the need for improvement and the impact of changed policies, it is essential to have meaningful community health indicators.

Recent decades have seen the development of robust systems of community health indicators, but those sets tend to neglect behavioral health. A community-based participatory research project in Austin, Texas developed behavioral health indicators after reviewing social indicators movements across the globe, proposed sets of key indicators of mental health and mental illness, and community initiatives in Austin relevant to behavioral health.

The community behavioral health indicators have been refined through the challenging process of implementing them in the face of competing efforts and imprecise communication about their use. Four indicators have been selected for which to identify strategies to effectuate, rather than just measure, systems change by engaging community partners around implementing a detailed action plan. While indicators must be adapted to suit local conditions, this indicator set should provide a good starting point for researchers and communities to assess and improve the behavioral health of their community and increase health equity.

This paper addresses all the conference focus areas at least in part, but in particular it describes an existing policy and programmatic mental health intervention that is based on the social determinants framework. Attendees will learn how one locality designed an intervention within the framework to produce and assess policy and practice change at the community level.

A Primary Prevention Framework for Mental Health: An Environmental Approach

Linda Shak, MSW

Prevention Institute, Oakland, CA. Co-author: Rachel Davis, MSW

Mental health is a critical component of an individual's physical health as well as the community's health. Sound mental health contributes to quality of life, enables people to care for themselves and others, and reduces the risk of other problems such as substance abuse, failing in school, and suicide.

Emerging evidence suggests that certain mental health problems can be prevented, or onset may be delayed and severity of symptoms decreased, through effective prevention and early intervention. Quality prevention requires a new way of doing business, expanding efforts to focus on organizational practices and policy change, reach out to new partners, and take a comprehensive approach to addressing the underlying determinants of mental health.

This session describes Prevention Institute's efforts in San Mateo County to develop "A Primary Prevention Framework for Substance Abuse and Mental Health" that emphasizes primary prevention and promotes mental well-being among all community residents. Primary prevention—taking action before the onset of illness— can support the care and treatment of those in need while also reducing the stigma associated with behavioral health problems.

Primary prevention strategies support equity by examining the role that the social, physical, economic, and cultural environments play in contributing to mental health problems and how those environments can be changed to prevent some behavioral health problems from occurring in the first place.

San Mateo's framework applies a social determinant of health approach by promoting social and environmental solutions to improve mental well-being, exploring factors such as community design, social connectedness, self-esteem/locus of control, violence prevention, positive early childhood development, and stigma reduction. The presentation will highlight the ways in which mental health considerations can be included in community planning and development and incorporate stakeholders working in sectors such as planning and community design/development, housing, transportation, economic development, education, and health.

4.3: INTERVENTION

Presenters: Fleda Mask Jackson, PhD; Gary M. McClelland, PhD

SUMMARY

During the Intervention session, Dr. Fleda Mask Jackson and Dr. Gary McClelland explained how to translate evidence-based research into meaningful knowledge that stakeholders can utilize to advocate for policy reform.

The session commenced with Dr. Jackson, a researcher affiliated with the Rollins School of Public Health at Emory University, who discussed The Measurement and Translation of the Social Determinants of Racial and Gendered Stress: Concepts, Measurement, Intervention and Advocacy. Research suggests that Non-Hispanic Blacks have a higher infant mortality rate in the United States when compared to Non-Hispanic Whites, and Hispanics. It is also suggested that African American college educated women are at a greater risk of experiencing infant death than non-college educated, unemployed, uninsured white women.

It is critical to understand these findings because pregnancy outcomes forecast future health status like increased risk of mental and physical impairment, poor health for the mother and child, and risk of future chronic diseases. Dr. Jackson realized it was important to understand the living conditions of African American women which contribute to adverse birth outcomes. Additionally, she wanted to understand how particular stressors of race and gender could be translated into interventions and policies to arrest the crisis of black infant mortality.

Dr. Jackson developed and utilized the Jackson, Hogue, Phillips Contextualized Stress measure to investigate the stressors of racism and sexism among African American women. The findings from the assessment of stressors of gendered racism revealed a link between anger, anxiety, and depression.

Equipped with the knowledge that social determinants are linked to health outcomes, Dr. Jackson proceeded to translate the evidence into feasible practice by developing interventions to curtail this racial health disparity.

When faced with gendered racism, Dr. Jackson recommended interventions like evaluating individuals perceived level of social support, developing a plan for self-care, developing a way to relax by engaging in a hobby, and avoiding drugs and alcohol. Furthermore, she developed Calming the Waters: Holding Back the Storm© for encouraging African American women to consider their strengths during stress-

ful events, and she developed the Save 100 Babies© campaign to advocate for more
equitable birth outcomes. From its inception, the campaign advocates several ways
to interrupt the black infant mortality rate – e.g., promoting healthy families, en-
during faith, positive social support, safe housing, healthy nutrition, quality education, fair employment, accessible transportation, and quality physical and mental
healthcare.

Dr. McClelland, a researcher affiliated with Northwestern University in Chicago,
concluded the session with Identifying the Institutional Bases of Effective Reform:
Lessons from Child Trauma. He advocates that the method of institutional history,
a method developed for understanding public policy and organizational behavior
in general, can be useful in understanding recent developments like the intersection
of mental health services and the juvenile justice system.

Dr. McClelland argues that successful reform must engage numerous institutional
domains like state executive agencies, state legislature, federal funders, courts, non-
government organizations, and professional organizations.

Dr. McClelland provided a case study to illustrate that successful reform requires
institutional penetration. He suggested that for the past thirty years, public sector
involvement in health care has eroded. Simultaneously, only limited populations of
youth in Illinois have received adequate access to health care. Data indicated that
96% of youth entering child welfare in Illinois have one or more measurable traumatic experiences and 80% meet the threshold for treatment. In the early 1990s,
individual estimates of the rate of mental disorders among detained youth varied
from 20 to 80%, which was a large discrepancy.

In 1995, The Mental Health Juvenile Justice Initiative (MHJJ), incorporated a strat-
ified random sample of detained youth, utilized a structured psychiatric interview,
and used a valid/reliable assessment instrument to establish an accurate baseline of
the epidemiology for youth in detention in Illinois. The MHJJ provided significant
empirical evidence that treatment reduced recidivism. Eventually, the state legislature mandated that all juvenile courts participate in MHJJ. This initiative expanded
into a state-wide program.

This case study emphasized that prior epidemiology and MHJJ program evaluation
altered the operations of the juvenile courts, implemented trauma-focused treat-
ments, and diverted youth from the justice system. Dr. McClelland concluded by
stating that both research and evaluation are critical to the policy process because

basic epidemiology stimulates policy reform, and program evaluation bolsters support. During the question and answer period, participants commended Dr. Jackson and Dr. McClelland for utilizing basic research and epidemiology to justify necessary intervention, advocacy, and institutional advancement in their communities.

SESSION 4.3 ABSTRACTS

The Measurement and Translation of the Social Determinants of Racial and Gendered Stress: Concept, Measurement, Intervention, and Advocacy

Fleda Mask Jackson, PhD
Rollins School of Public Health, Women's and Children's Center, Emory University, Atlanta, GA

In response to mounting evidence pointing to the link between the multiplicative stressors of racism and sexism and the physiological responses contributing to the disproportionately high rate of black infant mortality, a measure was constructed to assess the unique stressors confronted by African American women.

The Jackson, Hogue, Phillips Contexualized Stress Measure is the translation of the voices of African American women articulating the lived experiences of race and gender that were captured during focus groups and interviews.

The items on the scale comprise subscales designed to assess racism, burden (gendered stress), personal history of abuse and neglect, workplace stressors, support and coping. What the women gave voice to during the focus groups and interviews was those environmental assaults to their mental health and wellbeing experienced in the places where they gave birth, grew, lived their lives, worked and aged offering indications of the social determinants of mental health for African American women. Alongside their sharing of environmental stressors the women also indicated assets for coping and support to mediate racial and gendered stress.

The findings from the documentation and assessment of the stressors of gendered racism are revealing its link to anger, anxiety, and depression--- all risk for adverse mental and physical health outcomes. The results are also indicating the mediating effects of the coping and support mechanism deployed by African American women. As a component of the community-based participatory methodology employed for the research, the findings were translated into a model for research dissemination/intervention for community collaborators, Calming the Waters: Holding Back the Storms© and for a social determinants campaign for equitable birth outcomes, "Save 100 Babies ©.

This presentation will discuss key findings from the research and the ongoing process for producing evidence based cultural, racial, and gender specific intervention for wellbeing and advocacy for health equity for African American women throughout the life course and especially before and during pregnancy.

Identifying the Institutional Bases of Effective Reform: Lessons from Child Trauma

Gary M. McClelland, PhD

Department of Psychiatry, Mental Health Services and Policy Program, Feinberg School of Medicine, Northwestern University, Evanston, IL

Childhood trauma has extensive public consequences. Education, justice and child welfare carry much of this burden. These burdens are rooted in the biological and behavioral consequences of childhood trauma, including pervasive neurological and developmental effects and poor life outcomes (e.g., marital problems, substance abuse, and suicide).

For 30 years support for public sector involvement in health care has been eroding. At the same time, limited populations of youth in Illinois have seen their access to health care guaranteed by public institutions. These expansions of care are guided by the premise that childhood trauma underlies many public policy problems.

This paper develops an understanding ot the institutional foundations of these reforms and offers insight into how and why some youth are receiving trauma-focused services.

Institutional History provides a method to address these issues. Institutional history is a comparative method for systematically garnering evidence to understand public policy and organizational behavior. In July 2004 the Mental Health Juvenile Justice study began diverting youth with mental health needs from the justice system in six juvenile courts in Illinois. In 2008 the legislature promoted the study to a program mandatory for all juvenile courts in the state. In 2003 incoming governor Blagojevich appointed the Behavior Health Team to review policies and procedures in the Illinois Department of Children and Family Services.

A wide array of reforms followed, many focusing on childhood trauma and its consequences. Trauma centered initiatives are motivated by concern for children and adolescents and by organizational needs such as the desire to reduce the overall cost of juvenile justice. Early on, basic science and epidemiology are important to justify the changes. Demonstrated good outcomes are crucial as the programs move ahead. Institutional penetration is critical to the resilience and persistence of these programs. Trauma focused procedures implemented to guide the daily work of line staff, and involvement of multiple governmental and non-governmental institutions – courts, legislatures, advocacy groups – both enhance the resilience of these programs.

Artwork and Poster Presentations

Artwork Presentations

Portrait of the Faceless
Amanda Chan, BA
York University

A Dream Deferred
Raymond Mays
Habilitative Systems, Inc., Chicago, IL

Her Introspective Adaptation
Margret O'Reilly, MA
Adler School of Professional Psychology

Poster Presentations

Comparison of Catastrophic Impairment Health Coverage and Medicaid Waiver Program Policies for Acquired Brain Injury Survivors without Disability Insurance
Elena Ballantyne, BA
Adler School of Professional Psychology

Structural Analysis of School Policies that Mandate Physical Activity and Its Impact on Children's Mental Health
Jared Berger, MA
Adler School of Professional Psychology

VA Benefits: A blessing or another battle?
Madina Boyd, MA
Adler School of Professional Psychology

Social Emotional Learning: Leveling the educational playing field across socio-economic systems

Tracee Joy Francis, MASc
Adler School of Professional Psychology.
Co-authors: Scott Hoye, MA; Caryn Curry, MSW

Promoting Awareness through Action: The Social Exclusion Simulation

Kyle Handley, BA
Adler School of Professional Psychology

Incarcerated Mothers:
Importance of Prison Visitation Policies on Mental Health and Recidivism Rates

Ingrid Hogge
Adler School of Professional Psychology

Exposure to Community Violence for Drug-Using Southeast Asian American Youth and Young Adults

Juliet P. Lee, PhD
Prevention Research Center, Pacific Inst. for Research and Evaluation.
Co-author: Sharon Lipperman-Kreda, PhD

Maternal Responsibility or Maternal Stigma:
Controversies in Birth Defect Prevention with Female Alcoholics

Michelle R. Malalis, MPH
Rollins School of Public Health at Emory University

The Use of Institutions for Mental Diseases (IMDs) for Adults with Severe Mental Illness

Melanie Maxwell, MA
Adler School of Professional Psychology

Research Training Program:
Social Determinants of Mental Health Problems and Illnesses

Kwame McKenzie, MD
Centre for Addiction and Mental Health. Co-author: Heather Sanguins, MISt

The Family Leadership Institute: A Model for Empowerment with Homeless Families

Nicole Ranttila, PsyD
Psychological Consultations. Co-author: Christine Achre, MA

The Crisis in American Pediatric Mental Health

Andrew Schnell, BA

Adler School of Professional Psychology

Social Support and Depression: Examining a Social Determinant of Mental Health

Ruth Shim, MD, MPH

National Center for Primary Care, Dept. of Psychiatry and Behavioral Sciences, Morehouse School of Medicine. Co-authors: Peter Baltrus, PhD; Jiali Ye, PhD; Yvonne Fry-Johnson, MD; Elvan Daniels, MD; and George Rust, MD, MPH

Psycho-educational intervention for an indigenous community in Patzcuaro, Mexico

Tamara Sonabend

Adler School of Prof. Psychology.
Co-authors: Kristin Velazquez Kenefick, PsyD; Richard Ferguson, M.S.

"The Ten Names of Peace": Socio-historically Salient Metaphors and the Co-Production of PTSD in Bali Following Terrorist Attacks

Talia Weiner

The University of Chicago, Department of Comparative Human Development

Multicultural Competency:
The Synergistic Relationship between Wellness, Recovery and Resilience

Deborah Wilcox, PhD

Confluency Consultants and Associates

Pre-Conference Event:
Violence as a Social Determinant of Mental Health

SUMMARY

On Wednesday, June 2, 2010, the Adler Institute on Public Safety and Social Justice hosted the pre-conference "Violence as a Social Determinant of Mental Health" at the Drake Hotel in Chicago. This event was important for the American public because it highlighted violence as a critical social determinant of mental health especially in vulnerable communities.

The pre-conference explored the ways in which violence impacts mental health and how it can be mitigated. The event commenced with a keynote address by Dr. Carl Bell, Director of Public and Community Psychiatry at the University of Illinois. Drawing from his 30 years of research about violence, Dr. Bell promoted the use of community activism and awareness to address this important societal problem.

Following Dr. Bell, there was a panel presentation moderated by Anne Parry, the Director of the Chicago Department of Public Health in the Health in the Office of Violence Prevention. The expert panel included Erica B. Davis, Education Coordinator, Chicago Department of Public Health in the Office of Violence Prevention, and Marlita White, Chicago Department of Public Health and Chicago Safe Start Director. Consistent with the conference's theme "Awareness to Action," the panel presentation highlighted how Chicago-based violence prevention innovations, working across individual, community and structural domains, positively affect the mental health outcomes of local citizens.

The pre-conference event concluded with a Faces of Poverty Exhibit and Reception. The exhibit was a collection of photographs depicting the lives of Chicago's homeless population taken by Chicago Police Officers who are also M.A. Police Psychology students at the Adler School of Professional Psychology. Participants who attended the pre-conference enjoyed hearing the keynote address, the panel discussion, and viewing the photography exhibit. Participants commented that this event has illuminated violence as an important social determinant of mental health in marginalized communities.

THE FACES OF POVERTY PROJECT: EXPANDING AWARENESS & TRANSFORMING PERSPECTIVES

Presented by the Members of the Course, Social and Community Psychology
Masters of Arts of Police Psychology Program, Adler School of Professional Psychology

What does poverty look like? Do we recognize when we see it or do we turn a blind eye? Can we transform our perspective on poverty? The "Faces of Poverty" Project was a class assignment intended to blend creativity, self-reflection, community outreach, and public education in order to demonstrate how views of poverty can be transformed. The assignment was given to Chicago Police officers enrolled in a class examining the impact of social issues, such as poverty, on individual well-being.

The first purpose of the assignment was to provide these police officers with the opportunity of moving beyond a mastery of classroom material and actually engaging in a thoughtful examination of their own values and beliefs about poverty and the influence they have on how they see and relate to those who are the poor— particularly those they encounter every day in performing their duties.

This exhibition of the photographs and narratives of the Faces of Poverty by these officers is the second purpose of the assignment—to share their own process of discovery and transformation with others. You are invited to see for a moment through their eyes and to share with them their reflections on a social issue that touches all of our lives. I invite you to participate in their own process of personal transformation with the hope that it will challenge you to reflect on your own values and beliefs about poverty and perhaps encourage you to see it in a new light.

– Frank Gruba-McCallister, Ph.D.
Core Faculty, Adler School of Professional Psychology, Instructor, Social and Community Psychology

PRE-CONFERENCE SPEAKER BIOGRAPHIES

Carl C. Bell, M.D.

Dr. Bell is President & C.E.O., Community Mental Health Council & Foundation, Inc. He is also the Director of Public and Community Psychiatry and a Clinical Professor of Psychiatry and Public Health, University of Illinois. Dr. Bell is a co-Principle Investigator of the Chicago African-American Youth Health Behavior Project and of the Informed Consent in Urban AIDS and Mental Health Research Project, and a collaborator of the Chicago HIV Prevention and Adolescent Mental Health Project (CHAMP) at the University of Illinois. He is a member and Former Chairman of the National Medical Association's Section on Psychiatry; a Fellow of the American College of Psychiatrists; a Fellow of the American Psychiatric Association, a Founding Member and Past Board Chairman of the National Commission on Correctional Health Care.

During the past 30 years, Dr. Bell has published over 200 articles on mental health. He is editor of Psychiatric Perspectives on Violence: Understanding Causes and Issues in Prevention and Treatment; author of Getting Rid of Rats: Perspectives of a Black Community Psychiatrists; co-author of Suicide and Homicide Among Adolescents and chapters on: "Black Psychiatry" in Mental Health and People of Color; "Black-on-Black Homicide" in Mental Health and Mental Illness Among Black Americans; "Isolated Sleep Paralysis" and "Violence Exposure, Psychological Distress and High Risk Behaviors Among Inner-City High School Students" in Anxiety Disorders in African-Americans; "Is psychoanalytic therapy relevant for public mental health programs" in Controversial Issues in Mental Health; and "Prevention of Black Homicide" in The State of Black America 1995. Dr. Bell was the E.Y. Williams Distinguished Senior Clinical Scholar Award of the Section on Psychiatry of the National Medical Association in 1992. He received the American Psychiatric Association President's Commendation - Violence in 1997. He was appointed to the Violence Against Women Advisory Council by Janet Reno, the Attorney General Department of Justice and Donna Shalala, Secretary Department of Health and Human Services - 1995-2000, and was a participant in the White House's Strategy Session on Children, Violence, and Responsibility. He was appointed to the working group for David Satcher's Surgeon General's Report on Mental Health - Culture, Race, and Ethnicity, and was appointed to the Planning Board for the Surgeon General's Report on Youth Violence.

Anne Parry, M.A.

Ms. Parry has served as the Director for the Office of Violence Prevention at the Chicago Department of Public Health since 2001. She holds a Bachelor of Arts in Teaching degree from Trinity College in Washington D.C. and a Master of Arts in Social Science from Governors State University, Park Forest, Illinois.

Ms. Parry has worked for the past 27 years with Chicago children and their families in a variety of capacities: from Education Development Specialist to Executive Director. She has developed nationally acclaimed violence prevention community education programs Choosing Non-Violence.

Ms. Parry presents professional development courses on topics such as Stress and Violence, Understanding the Effects of Family Violence on Children, Gender Messages and Violence, and has authored books and articles addressing bullying prevention and caring for children in dangerous times.

Ms. Parry is one of the founders of Rainbow House, a domestic violence service agency based in Chicago. As developer of the violence prevention campaign known as TAKE TEN! Talk It Out! Walk It Out! Wait It Out! Parry demonstrates the creative and innovative approach she takes in her dedication to the safety and well-being of children and families. Named as one of Today's Chicago Woman's 100 Women Making a Difference, Parry is also a past recipient of Mayor Richard M. Daley's Local Hero Award and the Rainbow House Individual Courage Award.

Erica B. Davis, M.S., M.A.

Ms. Davis is the Education Coordinator at the Chicago Department of Public Health, Office of Violence Prevention is a trainer and the Education Coordinator for Chicago Safe Start. Ms. Davis' previous experience in child welfare and other violence prevention efforts have provided a vehicle by which her knowledge and understanding of the issues that impact children and families has increased.

Ms. Davis has been training since 1997 on topics related to family development, family violence prevention, school violence and bullying, domestic and teen dating violence, as well as, children's exposure to violence. She has presented at many events and conferences. Ms. Davis has been highlighted in a South Suburban newspaper as a participant in the Healthcare Consortium of Illinois General Assembly and a leader in Illinois' holistic health and education movement with Chicago Public School's Chief Officer of Specialized Services.

She is actively involved in the Chicago Police Department's Domestic Violence Sub-committees, as well as, other community organizations and area-wide task forces to raise awareness of the issues of the impacts of violence on children and their families. Ms. Davis is the lead author and editor of Bringing the Kids Back into Focus: Building a Community Response to Children's Exposure to Violence training curriculum, coordinator of the Chicago Department of Children & Youth Services (CYS) Making A Difference Training Initiative, Chairperson of the Making the Connection: Emerging Service Models for Children Exposed to Violence Summit, and team member of the animated teaching series, Stories for Children that Grownups Can Watch.

She has Master's degrees in Human Service Administration and Counseling and continually works to increase her capacity to provide effective training to a variety of audiences.

Marlita White, L.C.S.W.

Ms. White received her Bachelor's and Master's degrees in Social Work from Iowa State University in Ames, Iowa and the University of Illinois at Urbana, respectively. For 10 years, Ms. White provided and supervised direct services to high-risk and psychiatrically fragile children and families to enable them to remain safe and in the least restrictive treatment environment. She served as a quality assurance manager and consultant for multiple community mental health and child welfare programs managing accreditation, safe development, and projects to use available technologies to improve client care.

Since 1996, Ms. White has been involved in research, strategic planning, and program implementation for multiple violence prevention initiatives. As Director for the Chicago Safe Start program, she is a frequent presenter and trainer on topics related to young children's exposure to violence. She has contributed to as well as co-authored several written and video products. She oversees the implementation of the federal and local aspects including working directly on more than 15 boards, committees, and councils to engage child and family serving provider systems in improving their responsiveness to young children who are exposed to violence. Ms. White has been honored by the Federal Executive Employee Board of Chicago; she received the Dr. Martin Luther King Jr. Fellowship at the University of Illinois and the Outstanding Dedication to Children Award from the National Center for Child Exposure to Violence.

What's Next: Poised for Action

MENTAL HEALTH IMPACT ASSESSMENT TOOL

At the Adler Institute on Social Exclusion, we are building on the momentum of the conference to take "action" on the social determinants of mental health. Toward that end, in the future we will work to refine the process for conducting a Health Impact Assessment (HIA), which focuses explicitly on the mental health impacts of policy decisions and actions.

The HIA is "…a combination of procedures, methods, and tools that systematically judges the potential and sometimes unintended effects of a policy, plan, programme or project on the health of a population and the distribution of those effects within the population. HIA identifies appropriate action to manage those effects." (The International Impact Assessment Association)

Our work will advance the practice of HIA by expanding it beyond its traditional focus on physical health to include a greater focus on mental health and by moving beyond the mere assessment of land use and the built environment to consider a broader range of proposals, such as labor, education, and public safety, which are relevant to the needs of disadvantaged communities.

For instance, a Mental Health Impact Assessment (MHIA) can be used to evaluate the positive or negative impacts of public decisions on well-being. Clearly, neighborhood environments, living conditions, public service systems, and broader socioeconomic conditions like exclusion, racism, and distribution of income and wealth influence mental health.

The MHIA helps to ensure that public decisions impact social conditions in ways that promote mental well-being. MHIA will also boost community influence on policy actions that affect their lives; integrate health considerations into non-health decision-making; improve community cohesion, leadership, and capacity for coalition building and advocacy; and, highlight the inequitable impacts of policy decisions and actions.

The results of the MHIA will be used to provide evidence-based recommendations that mitigate negative mental health impacts, maximize positive health impacts, and increase health equity. We welcome your participation in these efforts.

HOW CAN I GET INVOLVED?

To facilitate your involvement, the Adler Institute on Social Exclusion is creating a Discussion Form. The Forum will serve as a venue for sharing ideas about the Social Determinants of Mental Health, and/or information about related best practices, noteworthy events and resources. This Discussion Forum will serve as a tool to "launch the global movement" of inter-disciplinary professionals committed to addressing the social determinants of mental health.

For more information on the Discussion Forum, contact the Institute on Social Exclusion at ISE@adler.edu.

Conference Sponsors, Credits and Contributors

SPONSORS

This conference is hosted and supported by the Adler Institute on Social Exclusion. For more information about the Adler School of Professional Psychology and the Institute on Social Exclusion, go to www.adler.edu or contact us at 312-201-5900 x311 or ise@adler.edu.

This conference is supported, in part, by the Robert Wood Johnson Foundation, The Kresge Foundation, and by the Substance Abuse and Mental Health Services Administration (SAMHSA), a division of the U.S. Department of Health and Human Services.

Robert Wood Johnson Foundation

THE KRESGE FOUNDATION

U.S. DEPARTMENT OF HEALTH AND HUMAN SERVICES
Substance Abuse and Mental Health Services Administration
Center for Mental Health Services
www.samhsa.gov

Credits and Contributors

ISE FACULTY AND STAFF

Lynn Todman, Ph.D., M.C.P.
Director, Institute on Social Exclusion

Lynn C. Todman earned a B.A. from Wellesley College and a Master's in City Planning and a Ph.D. in Urban and Regional Planning from the Massachusetts Institute of Technology. Her areas of interest are urban poverty and community development and the construction of social disadvantage. Her work draws on the fields of economics, political science, sociology, public health and systems' dynamics.

J. Sherrod Taylor, J.D.
Faculty Fellow, Institute on Social Exclusion

Sherri L. Boyle
Institute on Social Exclusion

Kerry Cochrane, M.A., M.S.W., L.C.S.W.
ISE Faculty Affiliate

Janna A. Henning, J.D., Psy.D., C.T., B.C.E.T.S.
ISE Faculty Affiliate

STUDENT CONTRIBUTORS

Elena Ballantyne, M.A.
Doctoral Student, Clinical Program

Jared Berger, M.A.
Doctoral Student, Clinical Program

Tracee J. Francis, MASc
Doctoral Student, Neuropsychology Program

This page left intentionally blank.

The Adler Institute on Social Exclusion

Made in the USA
Charleston, SC
06 November 2010